THE TRAVELS AND SUFFERINGS OF DANIEL SAUNDERS, JR.

DANIEL SAUNDERS JR.

CONTENTS

Introduction this Edition   v
Advertisement   xiii

1. Wednesday, 4th of May, 1791 departure from Salem   1
2. Saturday, 28th of April, 1792 departure from Madras   3
3. Tuesday, July 10 grounding off Oman's coast   5
4. Wednesday, July 11   8
5. Thursday, July 12   9
6. Friday, July 13   10
7. Saturday, July 14   13
8. Sunday, July 15   16
9. Monday, July 16   18
10. Tuesday, July 17   20
11. Wednesday, July 18   23
12. Thursday, July 19   25
13. Friday, July 20   27
14. Saturday, July 21   30
15. Sunday, July 22   32
16. Monday, July 23 arrival onto an island   35
17. Tuesday, July 24   37
18. Wednesday, July 25   39
19. Thursday, July 26   41
20. Friday, July 27   42
21. Saturday, July 28   43
22. Sunday, July 29 departure from an island   44
23. Monday, July 30   45
24. Tuesday, July 31   46
25. Wednesday, August 1   47
26. Thursday, August 2   49
27. Friday, August 3   50
28. Saturday, August 4   51
29. Sunday, August 5   52
30. Monday, August 6   53
31. Tuesday, August 7   55

32. Wednesday, August 8 … 56
33. Thursday, August 9 … 58
34. Friday, August 10 … 60
35. Saturday, August 11 … 62
36. Sunday, August 12 arrival at Muscat … 64
37. Monday, August 13 … 67
38. Tuesday, August 14 … 68
39. Thursday, August 30 arrival into Bombay … 70
40. Monday, 20th of January, 1794 arrival into Ostend … 72
41. Appendix … 74

INTRODUCTION THIS EDITION

This edition had been retyped from the original. Minor changes to the spellings used in the late 18th century have been made to make it a more readable text for 21st century readers. This includes changing the 'long s' to the modern 's'; removing ligatures between of 'c+t' and 's+t', modernising the spelling of places, Mirbat (originally Morebat), Muscat (Muskat), Mutrah (Matterah) & Mauritius (Isle de France) while leaving other place names unchanged (Bombay/Mumbai etc) where the previous name is well known. Regrettably no locations that were part of the land journey to Muscat were named.

Despite being written and published by in the United States of America, the original text has mostly British English spellings, which are current today. This is likely because of its own publication date falling between the issue in 1755 of Samuel Johnson's 'A Dictionary of the English Language', and Merriam-Webster's 'An American Dictionary of the English Language' (1828). The former sped up the standardisation of English spelling, while the latter simplified its spelling within the USA. The style of the text's construction, dating, numbering and punctuation is not so current. It uses exceedingly long sentences and paragraphs and no formal chapters; the style of the principal text is of a diary and flow of thought. This style has been kept , the dates of the journey have been used to create chapters, to aid reference.

Using terms within the text, such as 'savages' to describe the 'Bedoweens' (Bedouins), who gave the crew, food and water and ultimately rescued them is derogatory, though in the appendix he noted "The marks of poverty attended them - those especially whom we met with in the beginning of our travels." Indian Lascars (sailors) are interchangeably described as 'blacks' and Lascars, creating a thought there were two separate groups involved. Later he describes an Indian as a Moor of Bengal, presumably meaning Muslim of Bengal. However, in the narrative, as his situation becomes less desperate, Daniel Saunders terminology also change; he even notes, eventually, the name of one of his guides.

At the close of the American War of Independence (1775-1783), Daniel Saunders Junior lived in Salem, then among the ten largest towns in the newly independent United States. His father, also named Daniel, was a privateer - one of many fortunate men who had grown wealthy by capturing British merchant ships. Along the eastern seaboard, American privateers hunted the British trading vessels which had previously relied on the Royal Navy's canon for protection. However, the naval blockade of American ports, needed to protect Britain's Caribbean islands and hopefully cripple the American's war effort, had changed the Royal Navy's purpose. After the Franco-American alliance of 1778, and Spain's entry to support the American efforts in June 1779, and the Dutch in 1780, priorities again shifted. The Royal Navy was stretched thin with several Anglo-French naval battles in the Bay of Bengal, South Africa against the Dutch - and across the Atlantic and Caribbean Islands against France, Spain and the USA. Britain also had to defend its own island as enemy squadrons had appeared off Plymouth on Britain's south coast. The captains and merchants of Salem took full advantage of this distraction.

Privateering - or piracy, as the British government doubtless termed it - was authorised by the Continental Congress in March 1776. "State Maritime Courts" allocated the prize money due on captured ships. For Salem privateers, the risk of engagement was amply rewarded by the "prize" they secured. It is estimated that some 2,000 British ships were captured by a swarm of perhaps 1,500 privateers. A typical distribution for the crew's share was hierarchical: Captain (10 to 15 shares), Officers (4 to 6 shares), Able Seamen (1 to 2 shares). Daniel Saunders, though only a boy, must have known that a fortunate cabin boy in 1779 could receive $700 in cash - four years' pay for a soldier - alongside a ton of valuable sugar (*Saccharum officinarum*), thirty - five gallons of rum, and a share of commodities such as ginger (*Zingiber officinale*) and cotton. That boy was a wealthy, though potentially diabetic, teenager.

By the war's end, Salem was a seaport whose most valuable trade had evaporated. The Royal Navy, no longer tethered by the blockade, turned its guns toward suppressing privateers. During the conflict, the town had thrown itself into the fray with zeal; more than 150 Salem privateers had put to sea, the captured ships flowing into local wharves. These years trained Salem men in risk, rapid calculation, and the cold arithmetic of profit and loss. Peace in 1783, however, brought a loose confederation of states under articles that gave Congress no real power to tax, regulate trade, or enforce its own decisions.

Britain naturally reclassified the United States as a foreign entity. The Navigation Acts were enforced in full, excluding American ships from the profitable carrying trade between British ports. Simultaneously, shifting European alliances made neutral shipping alternately prized and risky. Sweden and Russia fought until 1790; Austria and Turkey until 1791; Russia and Turkey until 1792. From 1792, France was at war with a kaleidoscope of opponents. The War of Independence had taught Salem captains how to profit from conflict; the new era demanded they learn to profit from chaos.

The US Government's Tonnage Act of July 1789 imposed a modest fee of six cents per ton (a measure then reflecting a ship's internal volume) on American-built, American-owned vessels, but a much higher charge of fifty cents per ton on ships that were both foreign built and foreign owned. Vessels built in the United States but owned abroad were taxed at an intermediate rate of thirty cents per ton. It was a complex framework of charges - levied on every port entry by a foreign ship, and on each entry into American waters by a United States ship, or, if licensed, once a year. The effect was to stimulate the commercial trade of American-owned ships and to push foreign competitors to the margins.

A similarly discriminatory system applied to imported goods, with tariffs varying according to origin, route and flag. Tea brought directly from China or India in American ships paid duties ranging, by grade, from six to twenty cents per pound. The same teas, carried indirectly via Europe or in foreign vessels, were charged far more, with rates reaching up to forty-five cents per pound for the finest varieties. Layered together, these taxes made it increasingly profitable for American shipping to roam far and wide in search of cargoes and markets.

Alexander Hamilton persuaded Congress to take over much of the individual states' debt from the war and to rely on those customs duties and the complicated tonnage charges on shipping as the young federal government's main source of income.

To soften the immediate impact of these imposts, the new Treasury allowed duties to be "bonded": instead of paying the full amount in cash when a cargo entered port, an importer could lodge a bond and settle the sum in instalments over the following months, with longer credit extended on larger consignments. In practice, a careful but confident merchant could sell much, perhaps all, of a shipment before the bonded duties fell due. Money that was owed to the government could, meanwhile, be turned, by the risk accustomed merchants, to one more speculative voyage. The system favoured those who moved quickly and embraced calculated risks, above all traders handling high-value goods.

Salem was exceptionally well placed to exploit this new environment. In the first federal census of 1790 it ranked among the largest urban centres in the United States. More important than population numbers was the concentration of maritime capital and experience. Salem had yards that could build fast, seaworthy ships; it had a cadre of captains who had learned their trade, literally under fire as privateers; and it had merchant houses whose book-keepers had already grown used to juggling multiple currencies, distant markets and the uncertain timing of prize money income. Local wealth may well have been the highest per head in the new republic, a fact reflected in the brick mansions that began to rise behind the waterfront warehouses; these included Daniel Saunders own family's home, an imposing brick mansion on Salem's Boston Street.

Elias Hasket Derby, arguably America's first millionaire, pivoted from hunting British merchantmen to emulating them. In 1786, he dispatched the *Grand Turk* to Mauritius (Isle de France). When the market there for her provisions proved sluggish, French merchants suggested she sail to Canton. She returned to Salem in 1787, the first local ship to crack the China trade. The Indian Ocean, Derby realised, was a web of merchants waiting to be tapped. By 1789, he had four ships docked in Canton. Two had called at Bombay (Mumbai) - successfully navigating the route that would later prove disastrous for Daniel Saunders.

In 1791, Daniel Saunders sailed from Salem on the *Grand Sachem*, a 'snow' rig owned by John Derby the brother of Elias Hasket Derby. For Saunders, Mauritius was merely a transit point. Finding his situation "less agreeable than I wished," he transferred to the *Commerce* of Boston, captained by John Leach. Saunders effectively demoted himself from Second Mate to simple mariner on the *Commerce*, perhaps chafing under earlier discipline. Whatever the grievance, it was serious enough that Saunders resolved to abandon his coveted officer's berth mid-voyage and travel as a simple mariner.

Daniel's voyage aboard the *Commerce* began smoothly enough. Departing Mauritius in late January 1792, the ship crossed the Indian Ocean, arriving at the eastern Indian port of Madras (now Chennai) in the Bay of Bengal on 25 March. There she remained at anchor for nearly a month, during which time the vessel underwent a significant change of command: Captain John Leach departed, and the ship passed into the hands of Captain Samuel Johnson, a competent New England seaman, but one unfamiliar with the complexities of Indian Ocean monsoon sailing.

Saunders would later remark that the journey from Madras proved slow and frustrating - "the winds for the most of the time being contrary, and the weather boisterous, our voyage proved very tedious." It took forty-five days to round Cape Comorin and reach Tellicherry (modern Thalassery) on India's western coast - averaging little more than two knots an hour. Worse than the slow pace was the navigational misjudgment that followed. Saunders noted that "our Captain, being unacquainted with the coast, and considering the ship further to the eastward than she really was, steered more westwardly than he should." As a result, the *Commerce* was driven north by monsoon winds and currents streaming off the African coast, her true position misunderstood until it was too late.

On 10 July 1792, in the early morning hours, the ship struck a reef and grounded hard. Saunders believed, incorrectly, that the wreck occurred "near Cape Mirbat on the coast of Arabia." In fact, the geographical clues he provides in his journal suggest a different location. The coast near Mirbat is rugged and mountainous, with cliffs plunging into the sea and 100m of depth only a kilometer

(0.6miles) offshore. Instead, the stretch of coast around modern Al Jazir, further north, aligns more closely with his account having frequent shallow areas of seabed "Only two or three miles from the shore," he wrote about the ship's grounded location, "presented to our view a white sandy beach, the extent of which we could not see on one end or the other; and not a house, a hut, a tree or even a bush was to be seen." This location also fits with the number of days they took to reach, what can only have been, Muhut Island.

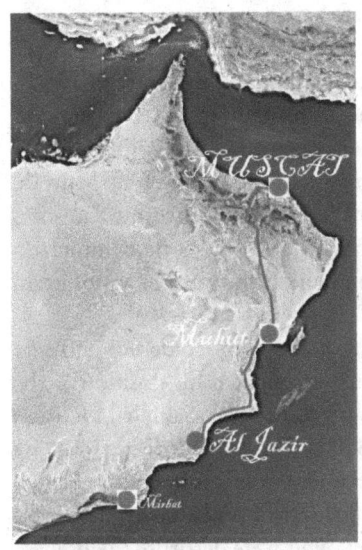

possible wreck location - and route north to Muscat

The crew came ashore in scattered fashion and regrouped. Taking little food and almost no fresh water, they set off northward, following the coastline toward what they hoped was civilization. The weather, it was during the mid - summer monsoon, will have been windy, with constant sand blowing and up to 14 hours of intense sun each day. The group frequently fragmented and reassembled. Men collapsed from exhaustion or illness, unable to go on. At least one was abandoned but then subsequently, independently, made the journey to Bombay. Saunders recalled one such moment with clarity: "he suddenly fell down on the ground; nor was he able to rise up again, or even speak to me: finding it in vain to stay with him, I covered him with sprays and leaves which I tore from an adjacent tree, it being the last friendly office I could do him. Thus I left him." That any of the crew met again was remarkable, given the absence of maps, the unfamiliar terrain, and the strain of survival.

Passing landscapes likely to be Ras Madrakah and the dunes of Ras Bintawt, the survivors eventually reached two islands - probably Rak and Muhut. Leadership had evaporated; the Captain separated from the remnants of his crew, and they failed even to cook fish or crabs. Relief arrived not from the sea, but on the padded feet of the ship of the desert. At Muhut, traders with camels (*Camelus dromedarius*) agreed to transport them. The starving men were packed atop the region's main export - dried shark (*Carcharhinus sp*) - and began the inland journey to Muscat on 29 July.

Their route curved through the arid heart of Oman. They passed several settlements - one of which may have been Sinaw, still today a market centre for inland tribes. At one point the caravan ascended a "prodigious high mountain." Saunders' language here must be weighed with caution; elsewhere he describes hills of perhaps a hundred metres as "mountains," so whether this was truly a mountain is uncertain. The group did, however, descend again toward the coast and finally followed the shoreline eastward until the city of Muscat came into view.

His description of Muscat, then effectively the Omani capital, is understandably admiring: "a large town; the houses well-built of stone, three and four stories high; it has a good harbour, and considerable trade; the inhabitants are numerous, and the place is plentifully supplied with provisions." For Saunders, Muscat was not just another port on the Indian Ocean rim. After weeks of thirst, hunger and uncertainty, it was deliverance into a safe harbour.

The Muscat that Daniel Saunders Jr entered in August 1792 was itself in the midst of change. For most of the eighteenth century, the political centre of Oman had been inland at Rustaq, on the edge of the mountains that Saunders had trudged past in misery. Under Hamad bin Said Al Said, however, the ruling family's seat shifted in the mid-1780s down to Muscat and its twin harbour of Mutrah, with their ocean-facing horizons and growing maritime trade. By the time Saunders arrived, the real business of rule - customs, diplomacy and sea-borne commerce - was being conducted on the waterfront rather than behind the walls of a mountain fort.

In March 1792 Hamad bin Said died during a smallpox epidemic and was succeeded by his uncle, Sultan bin Ahmad. Sultan consolidated his position at the coast while key strongholds were controlled by his brothers: one, Said, held Rustaq as imam; another, Qais, controlled the port of Sohar. Daniel had been travelling through a country with a minimally effective government that was in a state of great flux. That he received help on his journey - camels, water, protection - was good fortune: an indication that even the nomads he met, who were destitute themselves, would lend a hand to strangers.

Daniel's return to the USA was almost as catastrophic as his outward journey. He had travelled via Bombay, Mauritius, Madras, Calcutta, Cape of Good Hope, and in January 1794 arrived at Ostend (still part of the Austrian Netherlands). This was a rising port in northwest Europe that was consumed by the war declared by France on Britain in February 1793. Understandably there were no ships from Salem in port and while working out of the port he was 'press ganged' by a 'King's ship', presumably referring to the British King George III. He therefore effectively became a forced worker in the navy against which his own country fought in the American War of Independence until he escaped the ship and returned to Salem, in 1794, via Ostend - which was then occupied by France.

A Journal of the Travels and Sufferings of Daniel Saunders, shows the hardship involved in even successful trading voyages from Salem, the months on each leg of a journey is extraordinary. The disunity of the crew, despite being in the company of the Captain and one of the ship's owners (supercargo), suggests the difficulty managing a ship of the day must have presented. The text is valuable as much for what is omitted as for what was written.

The Travels and Sufferings of Daniel Saunders concluded on 20th of January, 1794 with his return to Salem "after an absence of about forty months".

An Appendix contains extensive quotes on Arabia, from *The Decline And Fall Of The Roman Empire* by Edward Gibbon, along with references to Constantin de Chasseboeuf, Comte de Volney's work and that of the geographer William Guthrie. The Biblical *Old Testament* is also referred to, illustrating Arab genealogy.

**THANK YOU 🙏 for buying this book.
I do hope you will enjoy reading it**

ADVERTISEMENT

It is almost unnecessary to observe, that the occurrences related in the following pages could not have been written during the painful Journey in which they happened. The writer, after his arrival at Muscat, noted down the events which took place from day to day during his travels, as he could collect them from his recollection of himself and his fellow sufferers, and by that means was able to form a connected journal from the time of the Shipwreck till his arrival at a place of safety; which he did solely for the satisfaction of himself and his friends. It's publication is in consequence of repeated solicitations for that purpose since his return to Salem. And he sincerely hopes, that no Mariner may ever have occasion to relate misfortunes and suffering like those which befell the company of the ship *Commerce*.

Salem November; 1794

CHAPTER I
WEDNESDAY, 4TH OF MAY, 1791 DEPARTURE FROM SALEM

On the 4th of May, 1791 I sailed from Salem, in the state of Massachusetts, in the capacity of second mate on board the 'snow' *Grand Sachem*, Jonathan Carnes, master bound to the Cape of Good Hope, where we arrived safe after a passage of one hundred and sixteen days, which brought it to the 30th of August.

Salem 1770s

We tarried at the Cape till the 9th of October, when we departed for the Isle de France, where we arrived on the 16th of November, all well. I remained with Captain Carnes can till the 25th of December, but having found my situation on board less agreeable than I wished, preferred going as a mariner on board the ship *Commerce*, of Boston, John Leech, master, which was then at the Isle de France: for this purpose I obtained my discharge from captain Carnes who received a man from on board the *Commerce*, in my stead.

On the 27th of January, 1792, we took our departure from the Isle de France for Madras, and arrived there safe, after a passage of fifty-seven days, being the 25th of March. Here Captain Leach left the ship, and Captain Samuel Johnson, of Rhode Island, took command of her.

CHAPTER 2
SATURDAY, 28TH OF APRIL, 1792 DEPARTURE FROM MADRAS

On the 28th of April, 1792, we sailed from Madras on the coast of Coromandel, bound to Bombay on the coast of Malabar, for which we shaped our course; but the winds for most of the time being contrary, and the weather boisterous, our voyage proved very tedious. On the 10th of June, to our great surprise, we saw Tellicherry on the Malabar coast, it being upwards of five hundred miles from Bombay; and the winds still continuing contrary, we tacked ship to the southwards, in order to cross the equator for the benefit of the southeast trade wind, to make our westing before we crossed the latitudes to the northward, the winds generally blowing along the coast from the southwest at that season of the year. Having stood to the southward until we reached the latitude between six and seven south, and having a fair wind, we then stood to the westward for four or five days, after which we altered our course northwardly, occasionally. On the 24th or 25th of June we fell in with the ship *Ganjava*, Captain Jemison, belonging and bound to Bombay, with whom we kept company for six or seven days, when we separated by some mishap, which proved unhappy for us, as Captain Jemison arrived in Bombay, in five or six days after. But our Captain, being unacquainted with the coast, and considering the ship further to the eastwards than she really was, steered more westwardly than he should have done. Nothing more of consequence occurred until the 10th July, when our misfortunes began. For five or six days previous to that time, we had had strong gales of winds from the southward and westward; and finding the water to be altered in colour, we were somewhat apprehensive of being near the shore. On the 9th of July our latitude by observation was 16°33'N, 58°E

Fort St. George Madras - mid 18thc Jan van Ryne

CHAPTER 3

TUESDAY, JULY 10 GROUNDING OFF OMAN'S COAST

Tuesday, July 10 - The same winds and weather continued. At eight o'clock, P.M. we tried for soundings, but found non with 120 fathoms line. At 12 o'clock, our captain being on deck, we sounded again, and found only thirty fathoms of water. Steering then N. and E. Our Captain, not at all alarmed, but imagining himself once more on the coast of Malabar, ordered the ship to be steered N.N.W. as he supposed for Bombay; but, to our great surprise, and greater misfortune, at three quarters past three o'clock in the morning, the ship struck the ground! The consternation we were thrown into by this unexpected shock the darkness of night which surrounded the dashing of the waves against our stranded ship - and the prospect of immediate death before us created a scene of horror past description! Continuing yet dark and in momentary expectation of the ship going to pieces, we waited impatiently the approach of day, which soon appeared, and in some measure alleviated our anxiety, when we found ourselves only two or three miles from the shore, which presented to our view of white sandy beach, the extent of which we could not see on one end or the other; and not a house, a hut, a tree or even a bush was to be seen. Having handed our sails, and finding the ship had not made much water, and the sea being considerably fallen, we hoisted out our boat, and carried an anchor out astern with the hope of heaving the ship off again; but that and every other effort proved ineffectual, nothing remained for us but to prepare for leaving the ship, and taking to the boats. We accordingly went to work to procure masts and sails for the boats, with provision, water, and as many other necessaries as the boats would conveniently carry. Our captain, in the meantime, with several of the hands went on shore in the pinnace, where they found twelve or fourteen savages but neither house nor habitation of any kind.

A 'snow' style ship - the Niagara

The gestures of these Barbarians indicated an inhumane and hostile disposition; and their conduct soon proved that it was not prudent to put ourselves in their power; for one of our people, who was less wary, or venturesome, than the rest, going within their reach, they immediately caught him and tied his hands; but he found himself means to disengage himself, with a knife which he had in his pocket, and returned to the boat. By this time everyone was convinced that we were not on

TUESDAY, JULY 10 GROUNDING OFF OMAN'S COAST

the coast of Malabar, but on the inhospitable shore of Arabia. Finding nothing on shore but what serve to augment or misfortunes, and add to the deplorableness of our condition, the captain return to the ship, and concluded there was nothing now to be done but to go to the boat as much to the advantage as we could in order to steer for Muscat. It being the nearest seaport on the coast that has trade with the Europeans. Having everything ready we really wanted, which are both would admit of carrying from the ship, we accordingly got them equipped with all possible expedition, and at three o'clock in the afternoon we got into the three several boats, being thirty-four souls in number, vis twenty Whites, thirteen Lascar sailors, and one African black. The ship by this time having bilged, her hold was full of water when we left her.

The order of leaving the ship was as follows:
In the Long Boat were,
Samuel Johnson, Commander;
Robert Williams, Merch't & Owner;
Nathaniel Seaver, Merch't & Owner;
Daniel Saunders, Mariner;
Gilbert Foss, do
William Leghorn, do
Soloman Buthby, do
John Daniels, do
And all the Blacks
In the Pinnace,
David Ockington, First Mate:
King Lapham, Carpenter
Valentine Bagley, Captain's Mate
Nathaniel Seaver, jun. Mercht's Son
Charles Lapham, Mariner;
Samuel Laha, do.
James Leatherby, do. and
Ebenezer Grant, do.
In the Yawl
Benjamin Williams, Cooper;
Thomas Barnard, Mariner;
John Quincy, do. and
John Rowe, do.

Leaving the ship, with the wind in the southwest quarter, we steered along the coast to the eastward till night, when, finding ourselves much fatigued, it being likewise hazardous to run in the night, we came to an anchor at a convenient distance from the shore. The water being somewhat smooth, and the wind light, we had a tolerable night's rest.

CHAPTER 4
WEDNESDAY, JULY 11

Wednesday, July 11. - Finding ourselves much refreshed by our night's rest, at four o'clock in the morning we weighed our anchors, and proceeded along the coast, with a pleasant breeze from the southwest, as before. At twelve o'clock we tried for an observation; but it being cloudy prevented our getting one to be depended on.

We continued our course along the shore until night, when we came to an anchor again in very shallow water, it not exceeding three or four feet; but being protected from the fury of the sea by a point that projected without the other part of the beach, we lay very securely all night.

CHAPTER 5

THURSDAY, JULY 12

Thursday, July 12. At five o'clock in the morning we weighed anchor again, and proceeded along the coast, wind and weather still favourable until three o'clock in the afternoon, when we stood off, to clear a long point that ran a considerable distance out into the sea; but the wind headed us so much that we could by no means clear the land; and the sea had by this time rose to such an height, that we could not venture upon the other tack without danger of being driven on shore by the surf; in consequence of which we came to an anchor.

Arab ship at anchor off Mirbat's mountains

The sea at length ran so high, that it was with difficulty we kept the boats above water; we therefore took the people out of the yawl, and let her drive on shore; the danger we were then in leading is to apprehend that it would not be long before we must follow her; our apprehensions and horrors increasing, as the boats began to drive towards the shore, and as we had no means left to prevent it, we were kept awake all night; but by good providence our boats kept afloat till another morning.

CHAPTER 6

FRIDAY, JULY 13

Friday, July 13. - Being reduced to two boats for the whole number, at day-light we made sail, in hopes to get out to sea far enough to keep our boats clear of the surf, which ran very high in shore; but every effort proved fruitless, we were obliged to put the boats before the wind for the shore, trusting to Providence to alleviate our misfortunes, and soften those hardships on the land, which we could no longer sustain at sea. Being now before the wind, which blew strong, and having a heavy swell, we soon got on shore in the long boat; and by God's assistance we were, every man, landed safe, being twenty-seven in number. When we had saved as many things as we could that were in the long boat, we stood upon the beach, waiting the landing of the pinnace, she being yet some distance off, and seemingly in great danger, being less qualified for encountering with the sea than our own boat. Our anxiety and apprehensions increased as she drew nearer the shore; nor were they without foundation; for, when she was about half a mile from the shore. We had the mortification to see her being before the surf, stern turned over head, which overwhelmed all that were in her, being seven in number, four of whom with difficulty reached the shore, and three were drowned viz King Lapham, Carpenter, Ebenezer Grant, Mariner and Nathaniel Seaver, jun. Merchant's Son. The grief of the father, who stood an unhappy spectator of this melancholy catastrophe, finding his son to be among the number of these who perished, may be more easily imagined than described.

Having saved some of our sails from the long boat, and the spars having drifted onshore, the morning being misty, we went to work to raise a tent, to keep ourselves as much as we could from the inclemency of the weather; which we soon effected. About nine o'clock the sun made its appearance, which afforded us an opportunity of drying our clothes, and other things we had collected on the beach, which came on shore from the boats. In walking the beach, we found a musket and powder horn, by means of which we kindled a fire, and made shift to cook a small pig that had swam on shore from the long boat: it proved a very delicious meal being the first we had to eat from the time of the ship's going on shore. Having thus refreshed ourselves and think we were pretty secure, not having seen a living creature since our landing, and being much fatigued, having had no rest the preceding night, we lay down to sleep; but, to our great surprise and misfortune, about three o'clock in the afternoon, we were alarmed by eighteen savages, on camels, armed with spears, cutlasses and knives, who rushed upon us, before we were aware of them; and, being in a very ordinary state of defence, we could make but a weak resistance: our Captain, however, & some others, exhorted us to defend ourselves, and protect our property; and in resisting them when they attempted to strip him, he received several slight cuts, but suffered no material injury thereby. Being in no condition to oppose them, they robbed us of everything we had, even stripping the shirts from off our backs; and to get from Mr. Seaver his hair ribbon, they cut off the hair close to his head. We importuned them, by signs and gestures, to leave us some old clothes to cover us, to prevent the sun from burning our skin; which, after some hesitation, they did, finding the spoil more than they could conveniently carry away; so that every man was left with some article of clothing: some had a shirt - some a jacket - some a pair of trousers - and one nothing but a strip of canvas to tie round him, except a hat on his head, which every man had, there being a number in a trunk which came ashore, and which the Arabs seemed to disregard. They now separated the Blacks from the Whites; and finding that the African (named Juba Hill, who came out of Boston cook of the ship) spoke the same language we did, they took him from the rest, bound him, and kept him; he crying to us in the greatest distress, to attempt his release; but this was entirely out of our power, and we expected every moment to be treated in the same manner ourselves, or to be instantly put to death if we made any resistance. Under this anxiety of mind, we laboured awhile, in doubt of what would be done to us; or what to do ourselves; at length we determined, if they seized on any one of us, to rescue him, or die in the attempt. Soon afterwards came three or four more Arabs, whom we supposed, by their appearance and conduct, to be some of their merchants who traded in the country; these assisted in collecting the spoil, and loading the camels with it. Having thus far waited the result of their proceedings with various thoughts and suggestions, about five o'clock in the evening, they permitted us, with the thirteen remaining blacks, to leave them, but not without sending two of their number, armed, as a guard, along with us, to see us to a short distance, probably conjecturing we might have something hid in the sand. When the guard left us, they informed us, as well as we could understand them, that we might travel to Muscat in five days. This, however, was far from being true, as we were then four or five hundred miles in a direct line from it, and the shortest route by land was doubtless twice that length: add to this, that our way lay through fields of burning sands, and over mountains of rocks and precipices, affording neither food to eat or water to drink exposed, naked, in the day time to a scorching sun, and in the night, to cold and heavy dews - and to the continual depredations of thieves and robbers - with no other guide, a great part of the journey, than the heavenly bodies, and the course of the sea - and without even the pity of man to soften our fate. Rejoiced, however, that these inhuman plunderers had quitted us, we began our wearisome journey, clothed with the remnants which the Arabs had left us, and in as good health as could be expected after our fatigues, excepting Mr. Seaver, who had been ill a great part of the passage, and was now quite weak, but who preserved a courage and firmness which gave , spirits to the rest, and did honour to himself. We travelled along the beach till dark, when, finding ourselves much fatigued, we lay down in the sand to sleep.

CHAPTER 7

SATURDAY, JULY 14

Saturday, July 14. - We arose again, and proceeded on our journey. About nine o'clock, we saw three Arabs, fishing, who seemed to show some fear at our approach, and a wish to avoid us: we passed them without taking any further notice of them. About an hour after, we observed at the head of the beach, several paths which seemed to lead into the country. We followed these paths some way, till we lost sight of the beach, and coming to a valley, saw some vines, which bore something very much resembling our watermelons, both outside and in; but on tasting them, we found them so bitter, that we could not eat them. There was now a difference of opinion, whether it would be better to keep on in these paths, or return to the beach and follow its course. Some were in hopes, that by keeping inland, they might find inhabitants, who would shew them more compassion than we had met with on the sea shore; while others apprehended it would be an imprudent and dangerous experiment, and were of opinion, that it would be best to keep along the beach, which tended to lead us most: to the eastward, and which was the course we were pursuing. Contemplating awhile on the circumstances, the Captain, Mr. Robert Williams, Benjamin Williams, Thomas Barnard, and all the Blacks, took the inland road; and the remainder of us chose to travel the beach. About noon, we saw three Arabs, fishing; we made what signs we could to them, to make them understand that we wanted water, and they walked along with us, until they brought us to a place where were two more of their fishermen: being now five of them in number, each having a large bludgeon, they went about to search if we had any money; finding themselves disappointed in that, they robbed us of some books and papers, and from one they took an old piece of canvas with which he had covered his nakedness; having done this, they let us go; and we proceeded on, without getting any water; after travelling some time, we discovered a spot on the upper part of the beach, that appeared as if there was water wanting to force its way up; we therefore began to dig and scrape as well as we could with our hands; having dug to some depth, and finding no water, we gave over the object, and betook ourselves to our journey again; but the sun being intensely hot, the sand scorching our feet, and having had nothing to allay our hunger, or quench our thirst the preceding nor all that day, it was with much difficulty the major part of us could walk at all.

Sea cliffs in mountains north of Mirbat

Providence at this time directing to our view a single Arab, we stopped him, and made him understand that we wanted water: he pointed us to the top of a precipice which was at some distance before us, where, as we understood him, we could find water: we accordingly hastened with all possible diligence toward the hill, and in a short time gained its summit,. Where, after some search we found a small well, which contained some brackish water; but being very thirsty, we drank our fill, and found ourselves much refreshed by it. After resting ourselves a little while at this place, we again resumed our journey, but had not walked far before we saw at some distance a number of men coming toward us, whom we at first took to be savages; but stopping a while to view them more attentively, we were happy to find them to be our own people, who had parted with us in the morning. Being once more joined in company, they informed us they had had water; and we walked all together down to the seaside again. Soon after, we heard a dog bark; from which we

SATURDAY, JULY 14

conjectured there must be fresh water at no great distance and looking up to the top of a small mountain, we discovered two dogs, but could not call them to us. This part of the coast being very mountainous, after some time spent in searching, we found a spring of good water, and having found some dry sharks bones upon the beach, where we imagined some of the barbarians had been eating some days before, we eat them, and having drank plentifully at the spring, we felt ourselves somewhat refreshed, as it was two days and a night since we had eat anything. It being now almost night, we walked to a rock we saw at a little distance, that hung over the beach and seemed calculated to afford us some shelter from the heavy dew that falls on that coast, under which we lay, in hopes to have some rest; but being so intimidated and frightened by the yells and cries of wild beasts, which, we supposed, came to the spring to drink in the night, we could sleep none all night. We knew some of these creatures to be jackals; but, from the different noises we heard, were fearful there were more dangerous animals among them.

CHAPTER 8

SUNDAY, JULY 15

Sunday, July 15. - At day light, we found some of the blacks were missing, and the remaining ones (excepting the captain's servant) parted from us soon after, taking the road to travel they most approved of: the rest of us continued walking the beach along until nine o'clock, when we ascended a mountain in hopes of finding water; having gained the top of the mountain, we saw. at some distance behind us, a number of savages, who seemed to be coming after us, in some haste; but not overtaking us, we conjectured they had gone another way. We continued walking across the mountain till twelve o'clock, but finding nothing either to eat or drink, nor the least prospect of getting anything, we divided ourselves, rather by accident, into three parties, each hoping to find a road that might bring them to something which might save them from perishing with hunger and thirst: Our party consisted of Captain Johnson, Mr. Robert Williams, Benjamin Williams, John Daniels,. William Leghorn, John Rowe, Thomas Barnard, James Leatherby, John Quincy, myself, and Manno, the captain's servant. Charles Lapham, Valentine Bagley, Solomon Buthby, Samuel Laha and Gilbert Foss, formed another party; and Mr. Seaver and Mr. Ockington, choosing to go by themselves, made the third. This was the last I saw of these two, and some of the others. The other parties left us, and went their way. We (being eleven in-number) saw at some distance a rock, whose head reached considerably above the other part of the mountain, and afforded some shade that would shelter us from the sun, whose heat was almost insupportable: under this rock we lay down until the sun had declined, and become somewhat more tolerable. About four o'clock we again proceeded on, and travelled until sunset, when we descended the mountain into a valley near the beach, in hopes of finding water there, but were unhappily disappointed. Finding no water, we ascended the mountain again. It being by this time quite dark, we lay down under a rock, which formed a kind of small cave, where we slept securely all that night.

CHAPTER 9

MONDAY, JULY 16

Monday, July 16. - At daylight we rose again, and proceeded along the mountain to the eastward, until about 9 o'clock. By this time the rays of the sun had become so intensely hot, and we so weak and faint for want of food and water, that it was with difficulty that any of us could walk at all; and Benjamin Williams, William Leghorn and Thomas Barnard, whose bodies were exposed naked to the scorching sun, finding their strength and spirits quite exhausted, lay down, expecting nothing but death for relief. In this deplorable, melancholy condition we left them, without being able to afford them the least help or consolation, nature calling for all our exertions to preserve our own lives. We therefore continued our journey, but not without being much disheartened and dismayed, at seeing our poor fellow sufferers, exhausted with hunger and fatigue, giving over the thought of living any longer, and resigning themselves to the arms of death. About an hour after this, Capt. Johnson and his servant left us, and took another way, more inland. The remainder of us (being now but six in number) still pursued our usual track, until near twelve o'clock, when we reached a shady place at the side of a rock, where we lay down till about three o'clock: we then got up, and proceeded on again until near six o'clock, when Mr. Williams, John Rowe and John Daniels took another way by themselves. The three of us that were left walked once more down to the beach, where we saw several old fishing nets, but nothing in them. Having been two days without a morsel of anything to eat, or a drop of anything to drink but our own urine or salt water, we grew very weak and faint: however, we walked on till night, and then lay down on the beach and went to sleep.

escarpment near Al Jazir

CHAPTER 10

TUESDAY, JULY 17

Tuesday, July 17. - At day light we rose again and proceeded on our journey. Having a long, hard, sandy beach to walk, the travelling was somewhat less painful than that of the mountains. About nine o'clock we met Mr. Robert Williams, John Rowe and John Daniels again, who, we found, had fared no better than ourselves. About an hour afterwards, we came to a rocky point that projected into the sea, about which we found many crabs and cockles, which afforded us great relief. James Leatherby now left us, and walked up to the mountain again, in hopes of getting water. The rest of us walked along the beach until about eleven o'clock, when, looking up to the top of the mountain, I saw Leatherby, and made use of some endeavours to persuade them all to go up to him; but they all declined, except Mr. Williams and myself, who parted with the rest of the company, and ascended the mountain as fast as we could, but could see nothing of him. When we had reached the top of the hill, Mr. Williams thought it was best: to keep the inland road, or rather find our road over the mountains. We descended the mountain, and travelled across a neck of land, which our companions upon the beach must have walked round, which shortened our distance considerably. We had not walked; far before we came to a mountain, on the sides of which we found large quantities of brimstone, which seemed to have been thrown out by an eruption. Passing this, we came to another mountain, on the top of which was a level piece of ground covered with a substance that appeared transparent, very much like icing-glass. We passed this also, and travelled until about one o'clock, when I became so weak with fatigue and want of bodily nourishment, and the sun so hot, that I could no longer support myself, and fell to the ground, and began to despair of ever rising again.

Coast near Al Jazir

But, by the blessing of God, my strength revived, and I was enabled to rise again in about half an hour, Mr. Williams having been so good as to stay by me during this conflict: when I rose, we walked down toward the beach, and I went immediately and bathed myself in the salt water, which afforded me great relief: then walking back to the head of the beach, I took off what rags I had on, and spread them to dry. Meanwhile Mr. Williams and I lay down under the rock, and slept for a while tolerably easy. When I awoke, I went down to the seaside, and caught a few crabs which afforded us a tolerable good meal. Although we found ourselves considerably refreshed, yet, so desperate were our circumstances, that I proposed to Mr. Williams to remain and end our existence at this place; but he having still some hope of getting to Muscat, we concluded to set out again. About five o'clock, we met Captain Johnson and his servant, who informed us that he had seen Mr. Seaver and Mr. Ockington, whom he left in a very low condition. Soon after, James Leatherby overtook us, and we all walked together till near sundown, when we saw a parcel of small rocks in a low, watery marsh, where we found a quantity of small fish in nets; but our mouths were so parched and dried for want of water, that we could not eat any of them. We imagined there must be fresh water near, from this being a place of fishing; and the Captain went back towards the country in search of some, and left us on the beach, to wait his return but it growing dark, and no appearance of his coming, we followed him, and walked until it was very dark, in quest of him. Now missing Mr. Williams, I returned in search after him, and found him asleep at the side of a rock. I awoke him, and we soon overtook our party, but could find nothing of the Captain. Having now nothing but our urine for drink, we lay down to sleep.

CHAPTER II
WEDNESDAY, JULY 18

Wednesday, July 18. - About five o'clock we began our usual hard labour, somewhat more inland; and, walking until noon, we met two women with a goat skin full of water; we importuned them some time for some of the water to drink; at length they understood what we wanted, and gave us about three pints of water each, and made us understand where we might get more. We immediately plied ourselves the road they directed us; and after travelling some distance, we met two men and six women, who at first treated us very hospitably, and gave us as much water as we wanted; they gave us also three small fishes each; but, our mouths being so sore for want of continual moisture, we could not eat them. Their thievish disposition now began to make its appearance; for one of the women, taking a fancy to Mr. Williams's shoes, went immediately and took them off his feet; they took from James Leatherby his shirt, and from me my hair ribbon; and, the men standing over us with large bludgeons in their hands, we durst make no resistance. Having gratified their curiosity, and taken from us whatever attracted their attention, they made signs to us to go away, which we did; and walking down toward the beach, we overtook the Captain, who informed us that he had got water, since he left us, of some of the Arabs; but that in return they had taken from him his trousers. We travelled along the beach until about 4 o'clock, when, seeing a number of trees and bushes, we went among them, in hopes of finding some water, but unfortunately found none. James Leatherby, Manno the Captain's servant, and myself laid down under a bush and tried to sleep, leaving the Captain and Mr. Williams to go on before us, as we could overtake them in a short time, being more accustomed to walk barefooted than they were, we having been destitute of shoes the whole journey.

Inlet from sea

Having laid about an hour, we got up again, and took the road the Captain and Mr. Williams had gone before: we travelled in this track over nearly three miles of land, the surface of which was covered with broken flint stone, which rendered our travelling very irksome and painful indeed. Having at length with much difficulty passed it over, we discovered, at a distance before us, Captain Johnson supporting Mr. Williams as he walked, who having lost his shoes, and not being accustomed to go without them, his feet were so tender, and so wounded with the stones, that he was scarcely able to walk at all: we soon overtook them; and not long after we met three savages with one camel: perceiving they had water on their camel, we made signs to them that we would be very thankful for a little of it; they accordingly filled us a cup that contained about a pint, which was all we could persuade them to afford us: this we divided among ourselves with a shell of a fish, which we carried with us for the purpose of drinking out of. The Savages then taking a liking to a jacket which the Captain's servant had on, they took it from him and went their way. At sunset we saw at a distance a number of wild date trees, which we went to, but not without much fear of meeting with Arabs among them; but not discovering any living creature there, we began to search for water, and soon found a small well, which appeared to have been lately dried up: we dug down some little depth, and found water; but it was very muddy, and proved of very ill consequence to us, our bodies being so empty that it went through almost instantly, as we drank it. Being now dark, we lay down and went to deep, where we rested without molestation that night.

CHAPTER 12
THURSDAY, JULY 19

Thursday, July 19. - At day light we began our course again over the mountains, there being a long neck of land projecting toward the sea, which would have lengthened our journey considerably by going round it. About nine o'clock, having gained with difficulty the top of the mountain, looking down to the beach, we saw an Arab,, fishing: finding no water on the mountains, we went down to the beach again, where the Arab was, and made him understand our necessity; and he was humane enough to take us to a valley where we found a spring of very good water. At this place we saw a great number of birds, some of which appeared like eagles, some were turkey-buzzards, and there were different kinds of small birds. Having drank sufficiently, the place being shaded with small bullies, we sat or lay down until about four o'clock in the afternoon - we then proceeded on again, and travelled along to the foot of a mountain. When we were at the spring, Mr. Williams's strength and spirits failed him so much, that he was unwilling we should leave that place when we did; and now he was so exhausted, that he fell considerably in the rear, and appeared scarcely able to walk, and almost insensible of his condition; and we concluded that it was not in his power to contend any longer with us against the hardships of the journey, more especially as there was no prospect of its having an end, nine days having already elapsed since our misfortune in the ship began, and not the least: appearance of drawing near Muscat, or any other place of refuge from the cruelty of the barbarians: we therefore with reluctance left him to the mercy of God, suffering ourselves all the horrors that fill the mind at the near approach of death.

Stunted, windblown tree south of Ras Madrakah

We then ascended the mountain, and travelled along it, until near sun set, when we descended it again, and walked down to the beach, where we found a quantity of crabs, which we eat, and I then walked some distance back from the beach again, where we lay down and went to sleep. In the fore part of the day some of the company were driven to the sad necessity of making use of a sustenance, to save them from perishing, too disagreeable to be named.

CHAPTER 13

FRIDAY, JULY 20

Friday, July 20. - At day break, we sat out again along the beach; but Captain Johnson's sinews and nerves had been so contracted by the sun in the day time, and chilled by the dews at night, that he found himself unable to travel any longer: he therefore concluded he must make his grave at that place, and told us that he could not wish us to make any delay for him, but advised us to make the best of our way along. We therefore took our leave of him, and left him in a similar condition to those we had left before; and a point we had to go round soon hid him from our sight. We travelled along till about nine o'clock, when we came to a grove of small trees and bushes, a little distance from the beach, where we found as many as a hundred and fifty people, who were constant inhabitants of this dreary abode, without a hut or roof of any kind, except what was formed by the trees, for shelter. Here was their baggage, their cooking utensils, and a great number of fish, which appeared to have been lately caught. In the midst of this grove was a good spring. Here we found one of our Lascar sailors, who had been at the place four days, and appeared to be in as good health as when he left the ship. The greater part of these people were women; & from the females we had met with we had commonly received kinder usage than from the men. They gave us as much fish and water as we could eat and drink, and even gave us fish to carry away; for which we thanked Heaven and our benefactors. Having refreshed ourselves greatly from this piece of good fortune, we found our strength considerably restored, and our spirits greatly revived; we then took leave of our hospitable friends, and proceeded along the seaside again, the Lascar choosing to remain behind.

Ras Madrakah cliffs and bay

About one o'clock, we discovered a man lying on the beach, with very little signs of life in him, and coming to him, found it to be Charles Lapham, in a most deplorable condition, having had no water since he left us, which was five days: we told him where he could get water, at about two miles distance: after many efforts, he got upon his feet, and endeavoured to walk: feeing him in so wretched a condition, I could not but sympathise enough with him in his sufferings, to go back with him, though it retarded my progress in my journey enough to do myself material injury, which both my other companions refused to do: accordingly, they walked forward, while I went back a considerable distance with Lapham, until, his strength failing him, he suddenly fell down on the ground; nor was he able to rise up again, or even speak to me: finding it in vain to stay with him, I covered him with sprays and leaves which I tore from an adjacent tree, it being the last friendly office I could do him. Thus I left him, and about an hour after, overtook my companions again. Travelling along the beach, about four o'clock we saw a man, a woman, and three children, of whom we got a little water, but not enough to quench our thirst. Leaving them, we walked until near sunset. Our travelling on the beach being obstructed by reason of the rocks running into the sea some distance, and very high, we ascended; the mountains again, on the side of which, we found a vast number of withered date trees, under and about which appeared to have been the habitation of some of the natives which was now evacuated. We found nothing here that afforded us any satisfaction; and, leaving it, we walked along the side of the mountain some distance, when, coming to a rock, whose craggy side hung over, and formed a sort of cave, we discovered two of our late shipmates, viz. Solomon Buthby and Valentine Bagley, lying down by a little stream of water that issued from the rock, which was the first they had found since their parting from us. We were happy to find each other yet alive, and concluded to travel together for the future, as long as it should please God that we should be enabled to encounter with the hardships of the journey. The mantle of day being now withdrawn, and night having spread her shades around us, we all lay down and slept tolerably well during the night.

CHAPTER 14
SATURDAY, JULY 21

S aturday, July 21. - At daybreak, we rose again, much refreshed by our night's rest, and applied ourselves to our daily toil and travel, being now five in number.

Crab (Ocypode brevicornis) Oman

We walked along together, relating to each other what had befallen us in the time of our separation; by which we found that Charles Lapham had been left by

Bagley and Buthby, the preceding day, in the place where we found him, according to their description. About nine o'clock, we very fortunately got some crabs and cockles, which proved a very seasonable relief: having eat as much as satisfied us, we lay down.

Among some bushes that grew at a little distance from the beach, the sun being so intensely hot, that we could by no means walk, or scarcely stand, and the sand had also scorched our feet in a shocking manner. Here we lay until about three o'clock. The heat of the sun being now somewhat more tolerable, and the tops of the mountains beginning to cast a little shade to the eastward, we sat out again. Leaving the side of the mountain, we had to travel across a neck of low land, which projected so far toward the sea that we could not see its extent, upon which we met two Arabs, who were good enough to give us water. We left them, and soon after reached the eastern side of the land, where we found it formed a deep bay, bounded by a sandy beach, which we walked till near five o'clock, when we met seven camels, with the same number of Arabs attending them. We endeavoured to obtain of them some information respecting the distance of Muscat, and understood them that they had been only one day from, thence. However we might misunderstand them, this created new spirits in us, and we began to think our greatest hardships at an end. We made them understand that we wanted something to eat and drink; and they gave us a handful of dates, which is a fruit that grows in that country, and preserve themselves when they are gathered ripe: this was all we could get of them to eat: they gave us a plenty of water to drink, for which we were very thankful. Being about to take our leave of them, they robbed Solomon Buthby of his hat, which it was not in our power to prevent, and then suffered us to depart. We followed the tracks of the camels over the mountains until it was quite dark, and then lay down upon a sand bank to sleep, when came an Arab, who surveyed us, and muttering something we did not understand, he left us, and we lay without further molestation all night, covering our bodies with the sand to protect us from the cold.

CHAPTER 15
SUNDAY, JULY 22

Sunday, July 22. - Awaking at day-light from our sleep, and finding ourselves much refreshed, and that we had derived considerable benefit from covering ourselves with sand, we once more began our daily travel, and walked till about nine o'¬ clock, when we found a well with very good water, where we drank our fill, and proceeded on our journey, still following the camels' tracks, till about eleven o'clock, when, finding we were going too much inland, we turned to the right hand again, in order to gain the beach once more, which we found very hard to accomplish, having most tremendous hills of sand to climb over, which appeared like mountains of snow; and the sand was so loose, that it gave way at every footstep, so that it was with great difficulty we could get over' them; the rays of the sun, and the' reflexion from the sand, being so hot, that it scorched our skins from head to foot.

Having at length attained the shady side of these hills, we lay down, and I believe slept about two hours. When we awoke, it being about four o'clock, we descended the hills into the valley seaward, where we fortunately found two huts, or small dwelling places, in one of which was an old man, in the other an old woman, who gave us a quantity of broiled crabs, which proved to us a delicious meal; but they could give us no water, having none in the huts, and the water of which they drank being at a great distance. After returning our humble thanks for what they had so hospitably afforded us, we took our leave, and proceeded down the valley until near sunset, when we met with two men who took us to an adjacent place, where they gave us as much water as we would drink.

Sand dunes Ras Bintawt,

After many signs and gestures concerning Muscat, they understood that we wanted to go thither, and agreed to provide camels and guides to take us there, for twenty-five dollars per man, making signs with their fingers to express the number, and calling the pieces of money *fluish*, which we found were dollars. It growing dark, we left them for the night, and walking to the side of an adjacent bank in the side of the mountain, we went to sleep.

CHAPTER 16

MONDAY, JULY 23 ARRIVAL ONTO AN ISLAND

Monday, July 23. - Early in- the morning we renewed our discourse with the Arabs, and agreed with them to give them their price to carry us to Muscat, in hopes on our arrival there to find some more Christian-like people, who would advance the money for our labour in their service, until we could clear ourselves of the bondage. Having got some water of the Arabs, about seven o'clock we sat out with one of them, who was to conduct us to an island, where were more of their company, who were to furnish us with camels for our journey to Muscat. Having walked down the side of the hill, we found ourselves on a white beach, the most beautiful to appearance that I ever beheld, the end of which we could not see to the westward; and taking our way eastward, we walked about seven miles, but could not see its end to the eastward. It was about two miles in breadth, and the surface of it as fair to look upon as a looking-glass, and so hard that the hoofs of the laden camels made no impression on it. At length we came opposite to the island we were to go over to, which was about two miles from us, and which it appeared almost impossible that ever we could wade to or near it, there being a very strong current running, by which we were in danger of being carried away, being so weak that we could scarcely walk the ground where there was nothing to obstruct us. However, our guide taking the water, at which he was very expert, we followed after; and wading through from two to three feet water, we at length reached the island, where we found near thirty more Arabs, unto whom our guide communicated our business; upon which they shewed us some signs of civility. Here we staid all day, without having anything to eat but a little salted shark, which is the most of their food; and there being no water on the island, we suffered much for want of it, especially in the excessive heat of the day. Late in the afternoon they gave us a little water, which was brought over to the island by an Arab, who was soon after followed by another, bringing Captain Johnson with him, in a very deplorable condition indeed, the sun having bred insects under his skin, which were destroying the flesh on his bones. Captain Johnson having fallen in with this Arab, he had agreed with him to give him fifty dollars to carry him to Muscat; and for that purpose he was brought to this island, as we had been. The sun having declined, the Arabs shewed us a cave in the island, where we retired and went to sleep.

Rak Island

CHAPTER 17
TUESDAY, JULY 24

Tuesday, July 24. -

Walkiing to Muhut island

At day light they made signs to us that we were to go to a neighbouring island, for the readier attaining to the camels when they were ready; and having the one for a guide that conducted the captain hither, we began our route, and walked a considerable way through soft mud, that had been created by the flowing of the water, which fatigued us very much, the sun at the same time having its full power on our heads.

We however at length reached the water, through which we had to wade about a mile, it being full three feet deep, which rendered it very difficult. But, notwithstanding our being so weak, by God's assistance we reached the shore we were plying for. This island we found very thickly inhabited, discovering at our first arrival as many as two hundred in number, who came down to the beach to meet us. The catching and curing of fish appeared to be the business of these islanders; and with their fish they carried on a traffic to Muscat. Our guide having informed them of our business, they received us somewhat civilly: they gave us dates to eat, and water to drink, of which we stood in great need, and from which we found ourselves much refreshed. But finding no kind of shade from the sun, we were very often in fear that we should die with its heat, it having blistered our skin from our heads to our feet; and our mouths were so parched, and our lips so swollen, that we could scarcely open them to admit of eating or drinking enough to keep us alive. Finding no shade to keep us from the heat of the sun (the savages not permitting us to go under their tents, or to eat or mix with them) we sauntered up and down the side of the island, not without being viewed and examined, as objects of curiosity, by the savages, who passed all day at intervals. Towards sunset they gave us some dates and water; and to lay upon, and cover ourselves withal, they gave us a large mat, in which we lay tolerably well all night.

CHAPTER 18
WEDNESDAY, JULY 25

Wednesday, July 25. - About five o'clock they awoke us, and gave us some dates and water, which we with difficulty swallowed.

Muhut Island

We walked or rather sauntered about the island the greater part of the day, to pass away the tedious time, which seemed to us to move very slowly. At noon they gave us sharks fins to eat, which they had broiled upon the fire, and water to drink: the remaining part of the day we passed as the former: at sunset we had broiled sharks fins, dates and water, and at night we lay down to rest, in the former manner.

CHAPTER 19
THURSDAY, JULY 26

Thursday, July 26. - When we a- woke in the morning, the Arabs brought us our usual fare; and the time seeming very tedious and irksome to pass, this being the third day of our being upon this island, and no prospect of the camels coming to deliver us from the burden we laboured under, we made signs to our conductors to know when we should go; and they gave us to understand that we should not go in less than three days, as they should not be ready for the journey in less time. They promised us we should fare every day as we had the preceding one, while we stayed on the island. The sun in these two last days had blistered our skins in so shocking a manner, that our condition seemed to be more deplorable than ever: we could not walk, nor sit or lie down, without enduring all the torment our weakness would bear. Thus we passed this day as the former ones, and at night lay down to rest as usual, but found ourselves very incapable of sleeping.

CHAPTER 20
FRIDAY, JULY 27

F riday, July 27. - In the morning the Arabs brought us our usual food, and continued as good as they had promised.

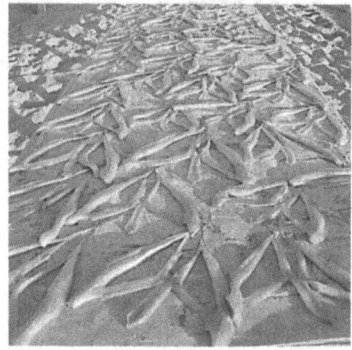

This day; passed as the former ones. The heat of the sun increasing our pain, our lives became a burden to us. Ending the day in the usual manner, we again lay down to rest.

Sharks flesh - cut and drying in the sun.

CHAPTER 21
SATURDAY, JULY 28

Saturday, July 28. - Attempting to rise in the morning, we found we could not stand, the flies in the course of the night having made holes in our skin, and filled them full of their insects, which made us so sore that we could scarcely endure the pain. Thus labouring under evils which grew heavier now than ever we had felt them before, we spent this day after the preceding ones, and at night lay down, in hopes the ensuing day to be removed, if it should please God to enable us to survive the night.

CHAPTER 22
SUNDAY, JULY 29 DEPARTURE FROM AN ISLAND

Sunday, July 29. - The day having appeared, we were called by the Arabs, who informed us we must prepare for our departure, there being a boat provided for carrying us over to the main continent, where the camels were ready to carry us to Muscat. We summoned all our strength together, and began our walk to the boat, where we embarked, but without receiving anything to eat or drink. Having reached within two miles of the shore, the boat struck the ground, nor would go any farther, the water being too shoal: we were all accordingly obliged to get out of the boat, and wade through the water, which was two feet deep. This was a task that from our weak and sore condition we were afraid we should hardly accomplish: however, with much toil and suffering we reached the dry land, being almost spent, the savages showing us no pity, nor affording us any assistance: but having with difficulty got on shore, they gave us some dates and water. Here we staid, waiting for the camels until three o'clock, when they came, being three in number, viz. one for the Captain, who had made a separate agreement, as before mentioned; and two for the rest of us, who were five in number; and each camel had a driver. The savages having laden the camels with salt shark they put us on the top of it, and began the journey, and travelled over the mountains till near sun-set; then stopped in order to let the camels feed: they made a fire also, and broiled some salt shark for us, and gave us the usual quantity of dates and water. It being by this time quite dark, we lay down to sleep.

CHAPTER 26
THURSDAY, AUGUST 2

Thursday August 2. - About three o'clock in the morning the Arabs called us, and we mounted to proceed on our journey, in hopes it was soon to have an end. We travelled, until about eleven o'clock when we stopped among a number of sand hills upon the mountain, where there was no screen from the sun; and the reflection of it from the sand hills, whose heads were so high that they deprived us of the benefit of the wind that blew, rendered it so hot, that it was with difficulty we could breathe as we lay down for we could by no means stand upon our feet. While we were at this place we saw three or four small girls and boys driving a large flock of goats, consisting apparently of several hundreds; but they did not come within two or three hundred yards of us. Having laid down some time, our man Ishmael brought us some broiled fish, with dates and water, which gave us some refreshment; after which, we lay down again till five o'clock, when they reloaded the camels, and set out again, and travelled till near one o'clock in the morning; when, coming to a number of bushes on which the camels feed, we stopped, and the savages unloading the camels as usual, we lay down among the bushes, and slept till about five o'clock.

CHAPTER 27
FRIDAY, AUGUST 3

Friday, August 3. - We proceeded on our journey again, and travelled until about eleven o'clock, the usual time; when, coming to a large well, where we saw between twenty and thirty savages watering a number of camels, we stopped; and of them we got some dates, all that we had being consumed; it proved a seasonable relief; and having drank our fill of water, we lay down until four o'clock in the afternoon, when we set out again, and travelled till about ten o'clock; when, coming to a thicket of bushes upon small hills of hard, sandy soil, this being a convenient place for feeding the camels, we lay down to rest for the remaining part of the night.

CHAPTER 28

SATURDAY, AUGUST 4

Saturday, August 4. - About five o'clock in the morning we continued our route again, and about nine o'clock we passed by a large grove of date trees, which were the first we had seen bearing fruit, and which encompassed a village, as our guide informed us, containing a number of inhabitants; but we did not go into it. Passing by this, we travelled until near eleven o'clock, when we came to a fine village, where we found the inhabitants very hospitable; it being surrounded by a number of date trees, whose fruit was ripe, they gave us a large quantity of them; and it being the first time, for a long while, that we had had an opportunity of eating our fill, we eat more than did us good; for it put us all in excessive pain the whole day. We staid among these remarkably civil people until four o'clock in the afternoon. Our men having laden the camels again, we were going away, when the friendly Arabs brought us a quantity of dates, which they gave us to serve us on our journey. We now set out, and travelled till about nine o'clock at night, when we stopped in the open road, without the least thing for shelter, where we lay down to rest, and spent the night.

CHAPTER 29
SUNDAY, AUGUST 5

Sunday, August 5. - About four o'clock in the morning we began our day's journey once more, in hopes we could not be far from Muscat, of which we were quite ignorant, as our guides would give us no satisfaction respecting it. Travelling till eleven o'clock, we came to a village that was evacuated, by reason of the date trees being barren. Our man Ishmael, with the other Arabs, leaving us here, with part of the camels' loading, they went to a large village which we saw at a distance, with some of the fish to sell, leaving us some dates to eat, and water to drink; which after we had eat and drank, we went into a house in this deserted village, that appeared to have been a place of worship, where we lay down to sleep; and our man not returning till near night, we were not disturbed until he came and brought two of our black sailors along with him, whom he had met with in his way. These sailors informed us, that the Arabs had circumcised Juba Hill, and sold him for sixty pieces of silver; but by what means they knew this, I cannot say. They stayed with us a short time, and then left us, appearing to be in pretty good health. Our guide having brought a large quantity of dates from the adjacent village, he gave us some, which we eat; and it growing quite dark, he informing us we should go no farther that night, we lay down again, and went to sleep a second time.

CHAPTER 23

MONDAY, JULY 30

Monday, July 30. - About six o'clock in the morning, the savages having laden the camels again, we proceeded and travelled till ten o'clock, when we came to a pond of fine water, where they unloaded the camels again, and mixed some fish with a sort of meal not unlike oatmeal, with water, and gave us to eat. After refreshing ourselves, and stopping awhile to let the camels feed, they loaded them again, and we continued our route, and travelled till near sun-set, when coming to a grove of trees, they delivered the camels of their burden, as they always did when they stopped; they then gave us our usual quantity of dates and water; and it growing quite dark, and this being a tolerably comfortable place to what some were which we had met with, we lay pretty easy all night.

CHAPTER 24

TUESDAY, JULY 31

Tuesday, July 31. - At two o'clock in the morning, the man to whose care I fell, and whose name we found was Ishmael, took one of the camels and went to an adjacent village for dates, and, returning about ten o'clock, brought a quantity of dates, and gave us to understand that in his way he saw one of our people almost dead; but having parted with so many, we could not conjecture who it was. Here we tarried till near sun-set, the day being so excessively hot that the camels could not travel; but the day being nearly elapsed, they loaded the camels, and we travelled till about eleven o'clock at night, when, coming to a level piece of ground on a mountain, where were a quantity of bushes on which the camels feed, they unloaded the camels as usual, and we lay down among the bushes and went to sleep.

CHAPTER 25
WEDNESDAY, AUGUST 1

W ednesday August 1. - About four o'clock the Arabs mustered us

Camels at rest

The camels being ready, we set out; and about eight o'clock, having descended the mountain, we came to a low marsh, which was covered with a strong, dry reed, which grew there as we imagined in the rainy season: we had to pass through this cane patch, and found it a very tedious undertaking: the tops of the reeds reaching the camels' bellies, retarded our progress in a great measure: however, about ten o'clock we had passed this troublesome part of the journey; and about eleven o'clock, it being so hot that the camels could travel no longer, we stopped in a place where we found three several springs; but the place we stayed in afforded us little relief, there not being the least shade or refuge from the sun. Our man Ishmael, going to one of the springs, caught twelve or fourteen small birds, which he broiled on a fire they had made, and brought them to us to eat; but one of the Arabs, begrudging us our meal, took some of the birds from us. From his freedom, we were encouraged to ask him: for water, which he as readily denied us. The water in the springs so near us not being fit to drink, our thirst and the heat became intolerable; not withstanding which, we were obliged to content ourselves until five o'clock in the afternoon when, having laden the camels, we mounted, again, and travelling, till about seven o'clock, we met seven camels, with the same number of savages attending them, whom we knew to be some of the people we had seen on the island the day of our landing there, and who had been to Muscat with the same kind of commodity that our camels were loaded with, viz. salt shark, and brought cotton and dates in return; the dates being their food, and the cotton they made their fishing nets of. We could not rightly understand how long they had been from Muscat; but we understood from them that there were a number of ships there, which gave us new life. Our conductors having exchanged some of the camels with them, we parted, and proceeded on till about eleven o'clock at night, when we stopped by the side of two fine springs, where were a number of savages, with twenty camels, watering. They gave us some dates; and having drank our fill of water, we lay down to sleep.

CHAPTER 30
MONDAY, AUGUST 6

Monday, August 6. - Having slept till about two o'clock in the morning, our man came to us, and informed us that the camels were laden, and waited for us: we accordingly hastened with him to the camels. Having mounted, we set out again.

Sinaw

About four o'clock, we passed by another village, and travelled till near ten, when we came to a very large one, containing a great many houses and stores, and vast numbers of inhabitants; the males, from the age of seven or eight years, to the oldest among them, being armed with spears, cutlasses, and long knives. At our first entering the village, we alighted from the camels, our curiosity prompting us to see the place, and being desirous to get something to eat and drink if we could find any among them humane enough to give us anything; flattering ourselves, that from the kind reception we had met with in the village we stopped in on the Saturday preceding, we should be civilly treated here also: but we were much mistaken in our suggestions; for, going among a number of them importuning them for something to eat they laid hands on us, and locked us, up in a house: we now began to reflect upon the indiscretion of our leaving the camels; not knowing what might be the result of our error, as we now found it to be.. Ruminating some time on our confinement, we were alarmed lest the camels and our guide should pass through the village, and, imagining we would follow them, give himself no concern on the occasion; but in a little time we had the pleasure of seeing him gain admittance into the place, and we were immediately set at liberty. Having now our guide with us, who we supposed had related our circumstances and condition to them, they gave us a quantity of dates, and shewed us many signs of civility. Our guide then took us to a marketplace, where we saw onions, dates, and vegetables of different kinds, for sale. They gave us each three pieces of copper coin, called *pice*, which is current in most parts of the East Indies; and some onions, which we eat with a good appetite. We tarried here till near sunset, when some of the inhabitants gave us some more onions, and a quantity of rice; they also lent us a pot to cook it in, which we looked upon as a great mark of their civility. Having eat our meal, which we thought a very good one, and night having darkened the sky, we laid down where we were, having no view of a better place, and slept quietly all night.

CHAPTER 31
TUESDAY, AUGUST 7

Tuesday, August 7. - In the morning our man came to us, and found us surrounded by a great number of the inhabitants, who were very desirous of coming near enough to us to touch and feel our skin, as they thought we were coloured with something that made us white having never before seen any people as white as we were, as Ishmael informed us. Having stood among the crowd some time, partly to gratify their curiosity, and partly because they were so numerous that we could scarcely get from among them, our guide took us to a man, whom we understood to be the Governor, or Chief, of the village, and who spoke the Moor tongue; and one of our Lascars being with us enabled us to satisfy the questions he asked us. He inquired of us, among other things, how long we had been with our man Ishmael, and how much we were to give him for taking us to Muscat: all which we informed him of; and he made a memorandum of it, in writing. Having gratified his curiosity, in answering his questions, he gave us dates, rice, limes, and onions, which afforded us an excellent repast. Having taken leave of the Governor, we went to the place where the camels were, and about three o'clock we left the village, and travelled till near nine, when we stopped among some craggy rocks. Our conductors having lost their way, knew not which way to go; and it being too dark to seek the right path, having given us some dates, and delivered the camels of their burden, we laid down till daylight should enable us to find our way out of this dreary place.

CHAPTER 32
WEDNESDAY, AUGUST 8

Wednesday, August 8. -
Early in the morning we renewed our course eastward; ascended a mountain, and descended it on the east side into a deep valley, where we met two women taking care of some goats which were feeding on the grass. These women informed our Arab's of the road which they must pursue, for Muscat. We left the women, and travelled through' the valley eastward, till it brought us to a spacious plain, in the middle of which stood a pleasant village, which we entered about ten o'clock, and found its inhabitants numerous and hospitable. They gave us plenty of dates, and treated us with much civility. They seemed much surprised at the whiteness of our skins, and were very curious in examining us from head to foot. We stayed here till three in the afternoon, much refreshed with our entertainment. The people in this village discovered more marks of industry, than any we had passed before, many of them being employed in preparing indigo, which they appeared to do with much skill and dexterity. We had now a prodigious high mountain to cross; and, alighting from the camels, as they could not climb it with us upon their backs, with many weary steps we at length gained the summit, where we overtook a number of men with asses laden with dates, going to Muscat, who had left the village we last came from a little before us. We soon travelled across the top of the mountain, and coming to the east side, the descent appeared almost impracticable, at its foot being a deep valley, and not a footstep or path of any kind to be seen, except a small, serpentine passage down the craggy sides of the rocks, which had been made by the fall of water in the rainy season: we took this passage, and, descending very slowly, with much caution and some timidity, we at length

reached the bottom in safety; and being much fatigued, the Arabs unloaded the camels, and, after eating some dates, we laid down upon the small stones and gravel that had been washed from the mountain, and slept there all night.

Date oasis base of Jabal Akhdar

CHAPTER 33
THURSDAY, AUGUST 9

Thursday, August 9. - About four o'clock in the morning we set out again, and travelled along upon small stones and rocks, about two hours, which brought us to a number of small hills; but finding no appearance of any path, our guides made a halt with the camels, and one of them left us to go in quest of a road that we might travel, but returned after a while unsuccessful. We then set out again, travelling eastward, as there was no prospect of finding a beaten path: after some time, we met an Arab with a loaded ass, going to some of the villages we had passed: he told our Arabs they were going wrong, and instructed them which way to take. Having accordingly altered our course, we soon met with another Arab, driving a number of camels to a village that had just at this time presented itself to our view thither we went with the strange Arab, where we found but a few inhabitants, situated under a long row of date and other trees. Here we stopped, and the camels were unladen, we going, as we usually did, among the villagers, to beg dates and water, or whatever we could get to eat and drink; we succeeded very well here, the inhabitants proving very hospitable, giving us plenty of dates and water. Having staid till about the middle of the afternoon, we left the village, and proceeded on our journey. About sunset we met an Arab on a camel, armed with a musket, which he carried (as we learnt from our man, who had a long discourse with him) to defend himself against thieves, who had lately committed many depredations thereabouts. This alarmed our conductors; and having parted with the stranger, we travelled with all possible speed till late at night, when we came among some rocks in a valley, where the Arabs concluded to stay the remainder of the night: they accordingly took the loading from the camels, and, having deposited it in the cavity of a rock, and put us as much out of the way as possible, in case of alarm, they left us, to take care of their camels. We then laid down to sleep, and neither saw nor heard any more of them till morning.

CHAPTER 34
FRIDAY, AUGUST 10

Friday, August 10. - About five in the morning we set out again, and ascended a mountain, more accessible than most of those we had passed. Descending it on the other side, a large plain opened to our view, after travelling in which some time, we came to a wide road, that appeared to be much frequented but our Arabs, judging, as we understood, that it was not the right road for us (though we afterwards found that they avoided travelling the direct road to Muscat, in order to prolong our journey, with a view of getting more money on their arrival at Muscat) they crossed it accordingly, and went to a village on the east side of the plain, which we found to be uninhabited, as we had found several before, from the same cause, the barrenness of the date trees. Walking through this place, disappointed at finding nothing to eat or drink, our dates (which were almost our constant food) and water being expended, we perceived, at some distance, a number of Arabs sitting in a circle on the ground; and, coming to them, we found they had a well of very good water in the centre; of which we drank plentifully, and filled the goat-skins, which the Arabs use to carry water in. After resting ourselves a little at this place, we travelled along the plain to the eastward, and soon came in sight again of salt water, and kept along the bank at the head of the beach a considerable time, meeting with a number of Arabs, men and women, with loaded camels, going into the country, and many others going the same way we were. At length we left the edge of the plain, and went more inland; and about six o'clock we saw another village, which we went toward, and met a young girl, who spoke to us in the Moor tongue, asking us whence we came, and whither going; of which we informed her: and she intreated us to go with her to the village, and she would procure something for our refreshment: she accordingly went back with us to the village, and immediately introduced us to a man, whom we found to be a Moor of Bengal, who had been cast away on the coast some time before, and, coming to this place, and finding the inhabitants hospitable and courteous, and desirous of his continuing with them, he had consequently remained there, and lived as comfortably as the country would admit of. We gave him an account of our misfortunes; after which, he went about to procure us something to eat; and soon produced a quantity of rice, dates, and onions, with bread, made of a sort of oatmeal, as we imagined, which was to us a great rarity, it being the first bread of any kind we had eat since our coming on shore in the long boat; for though we had seen it in some of the other villages, and begged for it as they were baking it at their fires, yet we could never get any. The Moor, and the girl whom we first met, having communicated our arrival and distress to some of their well-disposed neighbours, many of them contributed to our relief, in bringing provisions, of such kinds as they had, in so much that we could not eat half they set before us; which occasioned many of them, of whose victuals we did not eat, to leave the place dissatisfied, they thought they could claim no share in our thanks. Having eat sufficiently, and the Moor having related the manner of his being cast away, and how he had fared since he came to this place, he wished us much to stay with him till morning; offering us a place to sleep in, and telling us he would in the morning give each of us apiece of cloth to cover us, and procure us some good bread, it being so late he could get none that night; but his offers and entreaties were all in vain, for our conductors, suspicious that we might be induced to leave them to stay with the Moor, would not consent to our spending the night with him: we consequently parted with him and his friendly neighbours about ten o'clock, and walking a little way to one side of the village, we laid down and slept there the remainder of the night.

CHAPTER 35
SATURDAY, AUGUST 11

Saturday, August 11. - The Arabs awoke us very early in the morning, and having laden the camels, we began our daily exercise, and passed by two other villages before sun-rise, and coming to the edge of the plain just as the sun was making its appearance, we walked down into a valley of an easy descent, where we came to a rivulet of fine fresh water; and its banks being green, it made a most beautiful appearance to us, whose eyes had been so long wearied with the sight of desert sands, stupendous mountains, & craggy rocks. This rivulet, through which we had to pass, appeared to be nearly 100 feet wide, but not deep; and one of the Arabs going before, we all followed after, and crossed it with very little difficulty the water being about knee deep in the middle. We then travelled across the valley, and soon came to another rivulet, which we also crossed; and about nine o'clock we found ourselves at the head of the beach, which extended to the southward; and soon after, we halted at a grove of trees a little inland from the beach, it being a suitable place for feeding the camels: here we als0 received our usual portion of dates and water, and rested ourselves until after the sun had passed the meridian near three hours, when we set off again and travelled till late; and coming then to a thicket of small trees and bushes, close by the sea-side, after taking our usual fare we lay down to sleep.

Muscat 1870

CHAPTER 36
SUNDAY, AUGUST 12
ARRIVAL AT MUSCAT

Sunday, August 12. - Early in the morning we set out again, and travelled the beach to the southward. Soon after sun-rise, our Arabs, finding the beach was not the way by which we were to get to Muscat, once more altered their course; and travelling toward the mountain some time, we passed a small village; and about three hours after we discovered, as we entered on a plain, at some distance to the southward and eastward, a town, which made but a slender appearance, having only one house or building above the common huts: this house appeared like a place of worship, having a tower, with a dome on the top of it. As we drew near the place, we saw over the houses a ship's mastheads, whence we concluded it was Muscat. But its appearance seemed to afford us little hope of meeting with the succour or consolation we had promised our-selves, although the sight of a seaport gave us some relief, as we flattered ourselves, we might perchance find a European ship which would enable us to discharge the obligation we were under to our conductors. We plied forward for the town, and soon entered it, and, on inquiry, found it was called Muttrah. The inhabitants were very numerous, and flocked about us in great numbers to view us, until we came to the beach opposite where the ship lay, when we were accosted by a man, in the English tongue, who asked us many questions relative to our circumstances; and having told him our story, he informed us that he acted as factor for the English ships that came to Muscat to load, which had a safer harbour than Muttrah; that the chief of what he procured for the English was preserved dates, and small shells, which they call cowrie, and which are used for money in many parts of the East-Indies. We told him that we were concerned about getting money to pay the men who had brought us to this place: on which he proffered us what money we wanted, and said he was commissioned so to do. But he informed us that Muscat was not more than three miles distant, and that if we chose he would carry us thither in boats: we thankfully accepted his offer; and he accordingly hired two boats, one of which he went in himself, taking part of our company with him and the rest going into the other boat, we put off, and soon reached Muscat, having only a short neck of land to row round. On landing at Muscat, the Factor recommended us to the care of a man whom he met, and proceeded himself to the Governor directing the man, in whose care he had left us, to follow him with us. We soon arrived at the place of destination, where we were very well received by the Governor and his attendants. From there we were conducted to the house of a man, who acted as consul for the English, and who spoke the English language. This man, having heard our story, told us he would procure a ship to carry us to some English port in the East-Indies. He informed us that there were then two of our ship's crew in Muscat, besides us, under his protection, one white, man and one black. He then conducted us to a house, in which was a hall, where were a number of persons, whom we found by the Consul to be the magistrates and officers of the town, and who asked the Consul many questions concerning us, which he duly answered. We then went with the Consul to another house, which we imagined to be the bank, where he paid the Arabs, who brought us to Muttrah, 35 dollars, which was far short of what we had agreed to give them; but the Consul insisting it was enough, they took it and went their way. He next took us to a house near the seaside, where he ordered victuals and drink for us; and we were soon served with dates, fish, bread, and water. Having refreshed ourselves by this good man's bounty, and having a view of the ships in the harbour, we began to feel new life, and almost to think ourselves restored to our former strength & vigour, though' in reality we were still in a most deplorable condition. We were anxious to see our former shipmate, to know who it was that was so fortunate as to survive the journey, as well as ourselves; and soon after we found it to be Samuel Laha, as we saw him going in a boat on board of a ship. About 3 o'clock our attendants served us some rice, doll, and gee. The doll is a kind of grain very much like grey peas in England, which they split, and when boiled is tolerable food. The gee is a sort of butter, which they use as we do butter, but which Europeans and Americans do not much like. They gave us also some onions and dates: and having made another good meal, we felt our spirits greatly revived, though our strength was still low, and our bodies very sore. We now waited with impatience the return of the Consul, who had promised to procure us some clothes, as we were almost naked, and could not go out of the house on that account. He sent us a barber, who shaved us, and combed our hair; having seen neither razor nor comb since the time of our shipwreck till now. While this was performing, we had the pleasure of seeing our old shipmate, Laha, come in; who informed us, that he had been in Muscat four days; that he had suffered much in his journey, having walked all the way, without the least assistance; and that he was going to work his passage to Bombay in an English 'snow'. Having waited till near night for the Consul, we began to conjecture that he had forgot his promise; and it being late by this time, we were obliged to content ourselves for the night, and wait the result of the morning.

Muscat - late 19thc Lieutenant Colonel Charles Geoffrey Prior

CHAPTER 37

MONDAY, AUGUST 13

In the morning (Aug. 13) Captain Johnson sent a letter to the Master of the English 'snow' in which Laha was going to Bombay, acquainting him with our distress, and imploring his sympathy and assistance in contributing to our relief and in a short time after, an answer was returned by the generous Englishman, accompanied with several suits of clothes for Captain Johnson, and one for each of the rest of us. Having received so bountiful a donation from a man we had never seen, gratitude bade us make him the first offer of our services. The Consul came to us early this morning, and removed us to a house near the middle of the town, and told us he had clothes making for us. There was not an European or white man of any nation, in the harbour, who did not come to see us, so that we did not want for company the whole day: among other visitors was an Arabian, who commanded a ship that wanted a carpenter; and he took our carpenter's mate, Valentine Bagley, along with him, and put him into immediate pay, and gave him some very good clothes. The Consul took care to have victuals provided for us this day, as he had the preceding one: and about sunset we had the pleasure of seeing our benefactor, the Master of the English 'snow'; who came on shore to make us a visit, attended by his clerk, who appeared to sympathize with us. On offering him our service, he told us he was going away very soon, and advised us to slay on shore till we were stronger, and our health perfectly restored. We thanked him for his goodness, and he took his leave of us.

CHAPTER 38

TUESDAY, AUGUST 14

In the morning (Aug. 14) Captain Johnson applied to the Consul for money to purchase our provisions with, as we did not like the manner of the Arabs cooking it; to which he readily agreed, and gave him one dollar, adding, that if that were not sufficient, he might have whatever more he wanted. We now went to the market, and bought such provisions as we liked, and cooked them ourselves. Thus we lived two days longer; and finding ourselves much stronger, and thinking it advisable to get clear of expenses, if possible, we agreed to go on board different ships in the harbour to work, till an opportunity offered of going to some English port in India. I went on board an Arabian ship, where I found three French sailors, who were very kind to me, and gave me a shirt and trousers, which were very serviceable to me; and I stayed on board five days, and was well treated by everyone on board. On the sixth day, Captain John Christian Gaddis, of the ship *Laurel*, of Bengal, bound to Bombay, offered us a passage thither, which we all readily accepted, saving Bagley, who had gone carpenter in an Arabian ship. Capt. Johnson, Leatherby, Buthby, and myself, accordingly went on board the *Laurel*, and sailed the same night. Capt. Johnson gave us our bill of expenses at Muscat, for which he said he was responsible: it amounted to 11 dollars each, viz. for camels hire 7, one shirt and trousers 2, and provisions 2 more. But the bills were of little more consequence than to remind us that after all our hardships and sufferings we were in debt, and without a single farthing to discharge it with, or even to help ourselves.

Muscat harbour late 19thc

CHAPTER 39

THURSDAY, AUGUST 30 ARRIVAL INTO BOMBAY

On the 30th of August we arrived at Bombay, much recruited in health, thro' the goodness of God, and the unspeakable kindness of Capt. Gaddis and his chief officer. Thus, after a term of 51 days, in which we had suffered hardships and trials seldom known to human nature, snatched from the very jaws of death, thanks to the Supreme Disposer of all events, we were once more placed in a situation to seek a living in this variegated, troublesome world. -- On our arrival we found our old ship-mate Laha had got there before us: he came on board directly to see us, and informed us what ships in the harbour wanted hands; and Buthby went immediately on board the Queen, bound to England; but Leatherby and myself concluded to go on board the ship *Fame*, of Boston, Captain Standsast Smith, bound to the Isle de France and Ostend. This ship laid in dock at Massegon, a considerable distance up the harbour. We communicated our intention to Captain Gaddis, who approved of it; and calling us into his cabin, he gave us each five dollars; the Chief Mate also gave each of us one dollar, two shirts, two trousers, and one jacket: Capt. Gaddis's goodness did not stop here, for he hired a boat to carry us to Massegon; where having arrived, we agreed with Capt. Smith, and immediately entered on board his ship, which being then under repair, we did not sail until the 26th of September. On the 12th of November we arrived at the Isle de France; where I left Captain Smith, and took a third Mate's birth on board the American ship *Robert Morris*, Captain John Hay, bound to Madras; for which place we sailed on the 3rd of December, and arrived there the 9th of February, 1793; sailed again on the 25th for Calcutta, where we arrived on the 9th of March. Here, to my great joy, I was informed of the safe arrival of Mr. Robert Williams at Bombay, contrary to every expectation, considering the shocking condition in which we left him. On the 17th of March we dropped down the river, and on the 12th of June sailed for Ostend. On the 27th of September we fell in with a Dutch cruiser, with two prizes, bound into the Cape of Good Hope, where we all arrived together the 1st of October. Our ship being leaky, we tarried there till the 25th to repair.

CHAPTER 40

MONDAY, 20TH OF JANUARY, 1794 ARRIVAL INTO OSTEND

We arrived at Ostend on the 20th of January, 1794. Here the hands were all discharged, as the ship was going to England to repair. Finding no American ship there, I entered into the transport service, to keep clear of expenses till I could get a passage to America; and afterwards was pressed on board a King's ship, where I was kept several weeks, and then made my escape, and got to Blackwell in England, and thence back to Ostend; soon after which, arrived the 'snow' *Enterprize*, Captain William Ward, from Calcutta, bound to Salem; in which vessel I sailed on the 9th of June and arrived at Salem on the 17th of August following, when I had the happiness of being once more restored to my friends, after an absence of about forty months.

Soon after my arrival, I saw my fellow sufferer, Mr. Robert Williams; who informed me, that after we parted with him he went back to the spring we had left, where he caught Some frogs, and staid till he was a little recruited, and finally got along to Muscat; and that at Muscat he met with Mr. Ockington, whose unfortunate friend, Mr. Seaver, had failed in the journey.

Thus, out of 17 white persons who began the journey, I am knowing to 8 who got through & survived it, viz. Capt. Johnson, Mr. Robert Williams, Mr. Ockington, Valentine Bagley, Solomon Buthby, James Leatherby, Samuel Laha, and myself. The Lascars being always accustomed to going naked, and living abstemiously, it is supposed they suffered but little, and either got to Muscat or continued in the country, as they chose. It was the fate of Juba Hill, the black man from Boston, to be detained among the Arabs, probably as a slave.

Press Gang Clarkson Frederick Stanfield

CHAPTER 41
APPENDIX

APPENDIX.

The ship *Commerce* was cast away in that division of Arabia known by the name of the Happy Arabia - deriving that epithet from a luxuriance of soil which some parts of it possesses, unknown to the barren coast which it was our lot to travel. Scorching sands, moss-covered mountains, and naked rocks, were the painful variety which our journey afforded; and the people we met with had hearts as insusceptible of pity as the rocks of their coast. These people were of a swarthy complexion, and had black hair and eyes. The marks of poverty attended them those especially whom we met with in the beginning of our travels. The men generally had on no other clothes than a piece of cotton cloth about the lower part of the body, and sometimes a goat-skin turban on their heads; and were commonly armed: the women wore a long piece of cotton cloth, which covered them from head to foot, their feet being bare. They appeared to live mostly by fishing. When they gave us water at a distance from their springs, it appeared to be to them a precious article: more generous liquors they were probably unacquainted with, as they paid no regard to the wine which came ashore in our long boat. A grove of date trees was the habitation of some; others had tents, made with four poles set into the ground, and a mat fixed upon the tops; and as we drew near Muscat, we found numerous villages of small houses, crowded with inhabitants. Their food, their manner of cooking, and their domestic utensils, was as coarse and simple as their habitations; but these improved as we came among their villages; and it was observable that our treatment became a degree less savage, as we drew towards these settlements - a faint effect, probably, of the kind influence of society and commerce. When they robbed us, they never offered any violence to our persons, if we made no resistance. Muscat is a large town; the houses well-built of stone, three and four stories high; it has a good harbour, and considerable trade; the inhabitants are numerous, and the place is plentifully supplied with provisions.

ARABIA is in the quarter of Asia; and, as described by historians and geographers, lies, in its greatest extent, between the 12th & 35th degrees of N. lat. and the 36th and 61st of E. long. From its situation between the Isthmus of Suez, the Red Sea, the River Euphrates, the Persian Gulf, the Bay of Hormuz, the Strait of Bab Al Mandab, and the Indian Ocean, it may be looked upon as a peninsula, and that one of the largest in the world. Its first division, as we find by Scripture, was into Arabah and Kedem: Ptolemy divided it into three parts - Stony Arabia, Desert Arabia, and Happy Arabia.

As a great part of this country lies under the torrid zone, and the tropic of Cancer passes over Happy Arabia, the air is excessively dry and hot, A great part of it is a lonesome desert, diversified only with plains covered with sand, and mountains of naked rocks and precipices; nor ever, unless sometimes at the equinoxes, refreshed with rain. The sands of the deserts, when agitated by the winds, roll like the troubled ocean, and sometimes form huge mountains, by which whole caravans have been buried or lost. Wells and fountains are exceedingly rare. Those vast plains of sand are, however, interspersed here and there with fruitful spots, like so many islands in the midst of the ocean: these being rendered extremely delightful by their verdure, and the more so by the neighbourhood of those frightful deserts, the Arabs encamp upon them; and having consumed everything they find upon one, remove to another. The southern part of Arabia is blest with a fertile soil, which has acquired it the title of Happy: there are produced the valuable gums, which are carried to all parts of the world; rich spices and fruits, and corn and wine.

In Arabia stands Mount Sinai, memorable as the place where the law was given to the Israelites: at the foot of it is a beautiful plain, nearly nine miles in length, and above three in breadth, on which the Israelites encamped. From Mount Sinai may be seen Mount Horeb, where Moses kept the flocks of Jethro, his father-in-law, when he saw the burning bush.

The Arabs are distinguished by historians, as that remarkable people, of whom it was foretold, that they should be invincible - "have their hands against every man, and every man's hands against them". They have inhabited the country they at present possess, almost from the deluge, without intermixing with other nations. In the early ages, the Ishmaelites were one of the most considerable tribes in that country; and Kimshi, an oriental historian, insinuates, that they were originally the children of Hagar, by an Arab, after she had left Abraham.

According to the oriental historians, the Arabs are to be divided into two classes, viz. the old lost Arabs, and the present. Concerning the former there are some traditions, too unintelligible to be related here.

The present Arabs, according to their own historians, are sprung from Qahtan, the same with Joktan, the son of Eber; and Adnan, descended in a direct line from Ishmael the son of Abraham. The former of these they call the *genuine* or *pure* Arabs and the latter, the *naturalized* or *insititious* Arabs.

Joktan, the son of Eber, had thirteen sons, who sometime after the confusion of languages settled in Arabia, extending themselves from Mesha to Sephar, a mountainous place in the southeastern part of that peninsula. According to the Arabian historians, he had 31 sons, all of whom left Arabia, and went into India, except two, viz. Yarub and Jurhum; the former of whom, they say, gave the name both to their country and language, Ishmael and his mother Hagar, having been dismissed by Abraham, entered into the wilderness of Paran, as related in the book of Genesis. The sacred historian informs us, that during his residence in the wilderness, he married an Egyptian; and the Arabian writers say that he also took to wife the daughter of Mudad, king of Hijaz, lineally descended from Jurhum the founder of that kingdom. By the Egyptian, he was probably the father of the Scenite or Wild Arabs; and having allied himself to the Jurhumites, he is considered by the Arabians as the father of the greatest part of their nation.

But a particular history of the Arabs is aside from the purpose of this appendix. The propagation of a new religion, and the founding of a vast empire, by their countryman Mahomet, are subjects with which everyone is acquainted. Their national character is more in point; and this we may receive from the elegant pen of Mr. Gibbon - premising, that a character, which may apply to the nation at large, will undoubtedly be more favourable than one which might be truly drawn for the wretched inhabitants of a barren coast, separated from society, and living wholly under the wants of poverty, and the influence of evil passions - "On the seacoast: (says Guthrie) they are mere pirates, and make prize of every vessel they can master, of whatever nation."

The perpetual independence of the Arabs "has been the theme of praise (says Mr. Gibbon) among strangers and natives. The kingdom of Yemen, it is true, has been successively subdued by the Abyssinians, the Persians, the Sultans of Egypt, and the Turks: the holy cities of Mecca and Medina have repeatedly bowed under a Scythian tyrant; and the Roman province of Arabia embraced the peculiar wilderness in which Ishmael and his sons must have pitched their tents in the face of their brethren. Yet these exceptions are temporary or local: the body of the nation has escaped the yoke of the most powerful monarchies: the arms of Sesostris and Cyrus, of Pompey and Trajan, could never achieve the conquest of Arabia: the present Sovereign of the Turks may exercise a shadow of jurisdiction; but his pride is reduced to solicit the friendship of a people, whom it is dangerous to provoke, and fruitless to attack. The obvious causes of their freedom are inscribed on the character and country of the Arabs. Many ages before Mahomet, their intrepid valour had been severely felt by their neighbours, in offensive and defensive war. The patient and active virtues of a soldier are insensibly nursed in the habits and discipline of a pastoral life. The care of the sheep and camels is abandoned to the women of the tribe; but the martial youth, under the banner of the Emir, is ever on horseback, and in the field, to practise the exercise of the bow, the javelin, and the simitar. The long memory of their independence is the firmed pledge of its perpetuity; and succeeding generations are animated to prove their descent, and to maintain their inheritance. Their domestic feuds are suspended on the approach of a common enemy; and in their last hostilities against the Turks, the caravan of Mecca was attacked and pillaged by four score thousand of the confederates. When they advance to battle, the hope of victory is in the front, and in the rear, the assurance of a retreat. Their horses and camels, who in eight or ten days can perform a march of four or five hundred miles, disappear before the conqueror; the secret waters of the desert elude his search; and his victorious troops are consumed with third, hunger and fatigue, in the pursuit of an invisible foe, who scorns his efforts, and safely reposes in the heart of the burning solitude.

The slaves of domestic tyranny may vainly exult in their national independence: but the Arab is personally free; and he enjoys, in some degree, the benefits of society, without forfeiting the prerogatives of nature. In every tribe, superstition, or gratitude, or fortune, has exalted a particular family above the heads of their equals. The dignities of Shaik and Emir invariably descend in this chosen race: but the order of succession is loose and precarious; and the most worthy or aged of the noble kinsmen are preferred to the simple, though important, office of composing disputes by their advice, and guiding valour by their example. The momentary junction of several tribes produces an army; their more lasting union constitutes a nation; and the Supreme Chief, the Emir of Emirs, whose banner is displayed at their head, may deserve, in the eyes of strangers, the honours of the kingly name. If the Arabian princes abuse their power, they are quickly punished by the desertion of their subjects, who had been accustomed to a mild and parental jurisdiction. Their spirit is free, their steps are unconfined, the desert is open, and the tribes and families are held together by a mutual and voluntary compact.

"In the study of nations and men, we may observe the causes that render them hostile or friendly to each other - that tend to narrow or enlarge, to mollify or exasperate, the social character. The separation of the Arabs from the rest of mankind has accustomed them to confound the ideas of stranger and enemy and the poverty of the land has introduced a maxim of jurisprudence, which they believe and practice to the present hour: they pretend, that in the division of the earth the rich and fertile climates were assigned to the other branches of the human family; and that the posterity of the outlaw Ishmael might recover, by fraud or force, the portion of inheritance of which he had been unjustly deprived. According to the remark of Pliny, the Arabian tribes are equally addicted to theft and merchandise: the caravans that traverse the desert are ransomed or pillaged; and their neighbours, since the remote times of Job and Sesostris, have been the victims of their rapacious spirit. If a Bedouin discovers from afar a solitary traveller, he rides furiously against him, crying, with a loud voice, "Undress thyself, thy aunt (my wife) is without a garment." A ready submission entitles him to mercy; resistance will provoke the aggressor, and his own blood must expiate the blood which he presumes to shed in legitimate defence. A single robber, or a few associates, are branded with their genuine name; but the exploits of a numerous band assume the character of lawful and honourable war. The temper of a people, thus armed against mankind, was doubly inflamed by the domestic licence of rapine, murder, and revenge. In the constitution of Europe, the right of peace and war is now confined to a small, and the actual exercise to a much smaller, list of respectable potentates; but each Arab, with impunity and renown, might point his javelin against the life of his countryman. The union of the nation confided only in a vague resemblance of language and manners; and in each community the jurisdiction of the magistrate was mate and impotent. Of the time of ignorance which preceded Mahomet, 1700 battles are recorded by tradition; hostility was embittered with the rancour of civil action; and the recital, in prose or verse, of an obsolete feud, was sufficient to rekindle the same passions among the descendants of the hostile tribes. In private life, every man, at least every family, was the judge and avenger of its own cause. The nice sensibility of honour, which weighs the insult rather than the injury, sheds its deadly venom on the quarrels of the Arabs: the honour of their women, and of their beards, is most easily wounded; an indecent action, a contemptuous word, can be expiated only by the blood of the offender: and such is their patient inveteracy, that they expect, whole months and years, the opportunity of revenge. A fine or compensation for murder is familiar to the barbarians of every age; but in Arabia the kinsmen of the dead are at liberty to accept the atonement, or to exercise with their own hands the law of retaliation. The refined malice of the Arabs refuses even the head of the murderer, substitutes an innocent to the guilty person, and transfers the penalty to the best and most considerable of the race by whom they have been injured. If he falls by their hands, they are exposed in their turn to the danger of reprisals; the interest and principal of the bloody debt are accumulated; the individuals of either family lead a life of malice and suspicion: and fifty years may sometimes elapse, before the account of vengeance be finally settled. This sanguinary spirit, ignorant of pity or forgiveness, has been moderated, however, by the maxims of honour, which require in every private 'encounter some equality of age and strength, of numbers and weapons.

"But the spirit of rapine and revenge was attempered by the milder influence of trade and literature. The solitary peninsula is encompassed by the most civilized nations of the ancient world; the merchant is the friend of mankind; and the annual caravans imported the first seeds of knowledge and politeness into the cities, and even the camps of the desert. The arts of grammar, of metre, and of rhetoric, were unknown to the free born eloquence of the Arabians; but their penetration was sharp, their fancy luxuriant, their wit strong and sententious, and their more elaborate compositions were addressed with energy and effect to the minds of their hearers. The genius and merit of a rising poet were celebrated by the applause of his own and the kindred tribes.

The Arabian poets were the historians and moralists of the age; and if they sympathized with the prejudices, they inspired and crowned the virtues, of their countrymen. The indissoluble union of generosity and valour was the darling theme of their song; and when they pointed their keenest satire against a despicable race, they affirmed, in the bitterness of reproach, *that the men knew not how to give, nor the women to deny*. The same hospitality, which was practised by Abraham, and celebrated by Homer, is still renewed in the camps of the Arabs. The ferocious Bedouins, the terror of the desert, embrace,, without inquiry or hesitation, the stranger who dares to confide in their honour, and to enter their tent: his treatment is kind and respectful; he shares the wealth or the poverty of his host; and, after a needful repose, he is dismissed on his way, with thanks, with blessings, and perhaps with gifts."

BEDOUINS is a modern name by which the wild Arabs are distinguished, who inhabit the deserts, who live in tents, and who are perpetually removing from one place to another. Such is the situation in which nature has placed these people - under a sky almost perpetually inflamed and without clouds, in the midst of immense and boundless plains, without houses, trees, rivulets, or hills - as to make of them a race of men equally singular in their physical and moral character. This singularity is so striking, that even their neighbours the Syrians regard them as extraordinary beings, especially those tribes which dwell in the depths of the desert, and never approach the towns. When in the time of Shaik Daher some of their horsemen came as far as Acre, they excited the same curiosity there, as a visit from the savages of America would in Europe. Everybody viewed with surprise these men, who were more diminutive, meagre, and swarthy, than any of the known Bedouins: their withered legs were only composed of tendons, and had no calves; their bellies seemed to cling to their backs; and their hair was frizzled almost as much as that of the Negroes. They, on the other hand, were no less astonished at everything they saw: they could neither conceive how the houses and minarets could stand erect, nor how men ventured to dwell beneath them, and always in the same spot; but, above all, they were in an extasy on beholding the sea, nor could they comprehend what that desert of water could be. In general, the Bedouins are small, meagre, and tawny; more so, however, in the heart of the desert than on the frontiers of the cultivated country; but they are always of a darker hue than the neighbouring peasants. They also differ among themselves in the same camp; the Sheikhs, that is, the rich, and their attendants, being always taller and more corpulent than the common class: M. Volney has seen some of them above 5 feet 6 inches high, though in general they do not exceed 5 feet 2 inches. This difference is only to be attributed to their food, with which the former are supplied more abundantly than the latter. The lower class live in a state of habitual wretchedness and famine: it is a fact, that the quantity of food usually consumed by the greater part of them does not exceed six ounces a day: six or seven dates soaked in melted butter, a little sweet milk or curds, serve a man a whole day; and he esteems himself happy when he can add a small quantity of coarse flour, or a little ball of rice. Meat is reserved for the greatest festivals; and they never kill a kid, but for a marriage or a funeral. A few wealthy and generous Sheikhs alone can kill young camels, and eat baked rice with their victuals. In times of dearth, the vulgar, always half famished, do not disdain the most wretched kinds of food; and eat locusts, rats, lizards, and serpents, broiled on briars. Hence are they such plunderers of the cultivated lands, and robbers on the high roads: hence, also, their delicate constitution, and their diminutive and meagre bodies, which are rather active than vigorous.

The Bedouins have as little industry as their wants are few. They have no books, and are ignorant of all science. All their literature consists in reciting tales in the manner of the Arabian Nights Entertainment. In the evening they seat themselves on the ground; and there, ranged in a circle round a little fire of dung, their pipes in their mouths, and their legs crossed, they sit a while in silent meditation, till on a sudden one of them breaks forth with, *Once on a time* - and continues to recite the adventures of some young Shaik and female Bedouin: he relates in what manner the youth first got a secret glimpse of his mistress, and how he became desperately enamoured of her: he minutely describes the lovely fair; boasts her black eyes, as large and soft as those of the gazelle; her languid and impassioned looks; her arched eyebrows, resembling two bows of ebony; her waist, strait and supple as a lance: he forgets not her steps, light as those of the *young filly*; nor her eye-lashes, blackened with *kohl*; nor her lips, painted blue; nor her nails, tinged with the golden-coloured *henna* , nor her breasts, resembling two pomegranates; nor her words, sweet as honey. He recounts the sufferings of the young lover, *so wafted with desire and passion that his body no longer yields any shadow*. At length, after detailing his various attempts to see his mistress, the obstacles of the parents, the invasions of the enemy, the captivity of the lovers, &c. he terminates, to the satisfaction of the audience, by restoring them, united and happy, to the paternal tent, and by receiving the tribute paid to his eloquence, in an exclamation of praise, equivalent to *Admirably well!*

The Bedouin is a shepherd, without all the innocence of that character. The facility of passing rapidly over extensive tracts of country renders him a wanderer. He becomes greedy from want, and a robber from greediness. A plunderer rather than a warrior, he possesses no sanguinary courage; he attacks only to despoil; and if he meets with resistance, never thinks a small booty is to be put in competition with his life. To irritate him, you must shed his blood; in which case he is as obstinate in his vengeance, as he was cautious in avoiding danger.

Notwithstanding their depredations on strangers, among themselves the Bedouins are remarkable for a good faith, a disinterestedness, a generosity, which would do honour to the most civilized people. What is there more noble, than the right of asylum so respected among all the tribes? A stranger, nay, even an enemy, touches the tent of the Bedouin, and from that instant his person is inviolable. It would be reckoned a disgraceful meanness, an indelible shame, to satisfy even a just vengeance at the expense of hospitality. Has the Bedouin consented to eat bread and salt with his guest, nothing can induce him to betray him. The Bedouin, so rapacious without his camp, has no sooner set his foot within it, than he becomes liberal and generous: what little he possesses he is ever ready to divide: he has even the delicacy not to wait till it is asked: when he takes his repast, he affects to seat himself at the door of his tent, in order to invite the passengers; his generosity is so sincere, that he does not look upon it as a merit, but merely as a duty, and he therefore readily takes the fame liberty with others.

The unqualified liberty enjoyed by the Bedouins extends even to matters of religion. It is true, that on the frontiers of the Turks they preserve, from policy, the appearance of Islam; but so relaxed is their observance of its ceremonies, and so little fervour has their devotion, that they are generally considered as infidels, who have neither law nor prophets. They even make no difficulty in saying, that the religion of Mahomet was not made for them - " For (add they) how shall we make ablutions, who have no water? How can we bestow alms, who are not rich? Why should we fast in the Ramadan, since the whole year with us is one continual fast? And what necessity is there for us to make the pilgrimage to Mecca, if God be present everywhere?" In short, every man thinks and acts as he pleases, and the most perfect toleration exists among them.

THE END

THANK YOU 🙏 **for buying this book.**
I do hope you found it an interesting insight.
A review will help let others know if it's right for them.
It will also let us know what we need to improve.

www.ingramcontent.com/pod-product-compliance
Lightning Source LLC
Chambersburg PA
CBHW011317080526
44588CB00020B/2746